INsuccess

POWERED BY
GO Math!

INCLUDES

- Indiana Academic Standards Lessons
- Lesson Practice/Homework with Spiral Review
- STEM Activity Worksheets

Printed in the U.S.A.

ISBN 978-0-544-77896-2

6 7 0928 20 19 18

4500703039   A B C D E F G

Table of Contents

STEM Activities

Name _____

Relate Operations

Essential Question How can you use repeated addition to show multiplication and repeated subtraction to show division?

Learning Objective You will use repeated addition to show multiplication and repeated subtraction to show division.

 Unlock the Problem

When you **multiply**, you join equal-sized groups. When you **divide**, you separate into equal-sized groups or you find how many are in each group.

A train ride has 6 cars. Each car holds 4 people. How many people at a time can ride the train?

Use repeated addition or multiplication.

> **!** **ERROR Alert**
> Remember that the multiplication sign (×) is different from the plus sign (+). 6 × 4 means 6 groups of 4. 6 + 4 means 6 and 4 more.

This picture shows 6 groups of 4.

Add to find how many in all.	Multiply to find how many in all.
Write: 4 + 4 + 4 + 4 + 4 + 4 = 24	**Write:** 6 × 4 = 24, or $\begin{array}{r} 4 \\ \times\ 6 \\ \hline 24 \end{array}$
Read: 6 fours equal 24.	**Read:** 6 times 4 equals 24.

So, _____ people at a time can ride the train.

Try This! **Solve the problem.**

The roller coaster has 5 cars. Each car holds 3 people. How many people at a time can ride the roller coaster?

> **Math Talk** Which method do you prefer? Why?

Draw a quick picture to show the problem.

Use repeated addition.	Use multiplication.
Write: _____	**Write:** _____
Read: _____ threes equal _____ .	**Read:** _____ times _____ equals _____ .

So, _____ people at a time can ride the roller coaster.

🔒 Example Use repeated subtraction or division.

There are 12 people who want to go on the train ride. Each car holds 4 people. How many cars will be filled?

Subtract to find how many equal-sized groups there are. Start with 12. Take away as many groups of 4 as you can.

Count the number of times you subtract 4.

Write: 12 − 4   −   4   −   4 = 0

          ↑   ↑   ↑

    1 group   1 group   1 group

Read: From 12, subtract 4 three times.

So, 12 people will fill 3 cars.

Divide to find how many equal-sized groups there are. Make as many groups of 4 as you can.

There are 3 groups of 4.

Write: $12 \div 4 = 3$, or $4\overline{)12}$ with 3 above

Read: 12 divided by 4 equals 3.

Try This! **Solve the problem.**

There are 20 people waiting for the train ride. Each car holds 4 people. How many cars will be filled?

> **Math Talk** Which method do you prefer? Why?

✏️ **Draw a quick picture to show the problem.**

Use repeated subtraction.

Write: _____

Read: From _____, subtract

4 _____ times.

So, _____ people will fill _____ cars.

Use division.

Write: _____

Read: _____ divided by _____

equals _____.

Name _____

 **Share and Show**

Complete.

1. $6 - 2 - 2 -$ ____ $=$ ____

____ $\div$ ____ $=$ ____

2. ____ $+$ ____ $=$ ____

2 groups of ____ $=$ ____

____ $\times$ ____ $=$ ____

Draw a quick picture that shows the sentence.
Write the related multiplication or division sentence.

3. 5 groups of 6 equals 30.

✓4. $12 - 3 - 3 - 3 - 3 = 0$

✓5. $2 + 2 + 2 + 2 + 2 = 10$

> **Math Talk** A ride has 4 cars that hold 5 people each. How many people at a time can ride? **Describe** two ways to solve this problem. **Explain** how the two ways are related.

On Your Own

Draw a quick picture that shows the sentence.
Write the related multiplication or division sentence.

6. $14 - 7 - 7 = 0$

7. $4 + 4 + 4 = 12$

8. 2 groups of 9 equals 18.

GO DEEPER **Tell whether the number sentence is** *true* **or** *false*.
Explain how you know.

9. $8 + 8 + 8 \overset{?}{=} 3 \times 8$

10. $3 \times 7 \overset{?}{=} 14 + 7$

11. $5 \times 4 \overset{?}{=} 4 + 4 + 4 + 4$

🔑 Unlock the Problem

12. The Scrambler ride holds 27 people. Each car holds 3 people. If 7 cars are full and the rest of the cars are empty, how many more people can get on the Scrambler ride?

(A) 6   (B) 9   (C) 10   (D) 21

a. What do you need to know?

_____

b. What operation would you use to find the number of people on the Scrambler?

_____

c. What operation would you use to find how many more people can get on the Scrambler?

_____

d. Show the steps you use to solve the problem.

e. Complete the sentences.

The Scrambler can hold _____ people.

There are _____ people on the Scrambler.

The number of people who can still get on

the Scrambler is _____.

f. Fill in the bubble for the correct answer choice above.

---

13. Which of these is another way to write
$21 - 7 - 7 - 7 = 0$?

(A) $21 \div 7 = 3$

(B) $21 \div 3 = 7$

(C) $7 \times 3 = 21$

(D) $7 + 7 + 7 + 7 = 21$

14. There are 24 people waiting for the Ferris wheel. Each car will hold 4 people. How many cars will be filled?

(A) 4

(B) 6

(C) 18

(D) 30

Relate Operations

Learning Objective You will use repeated addition to show multiplication and repeated subtraction to show division.

**Write the related multiplication or division sentence.
Draw a quick picture that shows the sentence.**

1. $3 + 3 + 3 + 3 = 12$

_____$4 \times 3 = 12$_____

2. $18 - 6 - 6 - 6 = 0$

_____

3. 5 groups of 5 equals 25

_____

4. 24 among 4 groups equals 6

_____

5. $7 + 7 + 7 = 21$

_____

6. $32 - 8 - 8 - 8 - 8 = 0$

_____

7. $36 - 9 - 9 - 9 - 9 = 0$

_____

8. 4 groups of 7 equals 28

_____

9. $8 + 8 + 8 = 24$

_____

Problem Solving Real World

10. Courtney is pouring 18 cups of lemonade into glasses. Each glass holds 2 cups of lemonade. How many glasses will Courtney fill?

_____

11. It costs 6 tickets to ride the Ferris wheel. The ride operator collected tickets from 7 children. How many tickets did the ride operator collect in all?

_____

Lesson Check

1. Which of these is another way to write $9 + 9 + 9 + 9 = 36$?

   (A) $36 \div 4 = 9$

   (B) $4 \times 9 = 36$

   (C) $4 + 9 = 13$

   (D) $36 \div 6 = 6$

2. Martin has 18 craft sticks for making puppets. Each puppet is made with 3 craft sticks. How many puppets can Martin make?

   (A) 3

   (B) 6

   (C) 9

   (D) 15

Spiral Review

3. What is the value of the digit 7 in the number 379,120?

   (A) 7

   (B) 7,000

   (C) 70,000

   (D) 700,000

4. How many ten thousands are in 1,000,000?

   (A) 10

   (B) 100

   (C) 1,000

   (D) 10,000

5. Three children ride tricycles, and each tricycle has 3 wheels. How many wheels do the tricycles have all together?

6. Tomas has a rope that is 10 feet long. He cuts the rope into 2-foot sections. How many sections of rope does Tomas make?

Name _____

Model Equal Groups

Essential Question How can you use models to solve multiplication or division problems?

Learning Objective You will use models to solve multiplication and division problems.

🔑 Unlock the Problem 🌐 Real World

You can make models or draw pictures to solve multiplication and division problems.

🔓 One Way Draw equal-sized groups.

A A barbecue stand at the school picnic has 3 tables. There are 4 seats at each table. How many seats are there at the tables?

COMPLETE THE MODEL	THINK	RECORD
	_____ tables	4 ← **factor**
	_____ seats at each table	× 3 ← factor
	_____ seats in all	12 ← **product**

So, there are 12 seats at the tables.

B A barbecue stand at the picnic has 12 seats. There are 4 seats at each table. How many tables are at the stand?

COMPLETE THE MODEL	THINK	RECORD
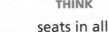	_____ seats in all	$12 \div 4 = 3$ or $4\overline{)12}^{\;3}$
	_____ seats at each table	↑ ↑ ↑
	_____ tables	**dividend** **divisor** **quotient**

So, there are 3 tables at the stand.

Try This! **What if** there are 12 seats and 3 tables? How many seats are at each table?

MODEL	THINK	RECORD
Draw equal-sized groups.	_____ seats in all	
	_____ tables	
	_____ seats at each table	_____

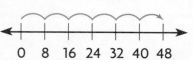 Another Way Use a number line.

A Mice can move at speeds up to 8 miles per hour. Horses can move up to 6 times as fast. How fast can horses move?

COMPLETE THE MODEL

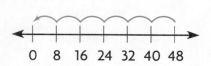

0 8 16 24 32 40 48

THINK

_____ jumps of _____

_____ miles per hour in all

RECORD

6 ← factor
×8 ← factor
48 ← product

So, horses can move at speeds up to 48 miles per hour.

B Mice can move at speeds up to 8 miles per hour, and horses can move at speeds up to 48 miles per hour. How many times faster can horses move than mice?

COMPLETE THE MODEL

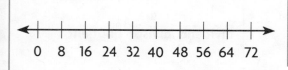

0 8 16 24 32 40 48

THINK

_____ times faster

_____ jumps of _____

RECORD

48 ÷ 8 = 6 or 8)48̄ (quotient 6)

↑   ↑   ↑
dividend divisor quotient

So, horses can move up to 6 times as fast as mice.

Try This! **What if** a horse moved at a speed of 8 miles per hour without stopping? How many hours would it take the horse to travel 72 miles?

COMPLETE THE MODEL

Use a number line.

0 8 16 24 32 40 48 56 64 72

THINK

_____ hours in all

_____ jumps of _____

RECORD

_____

So, it would take the horse _____ hours to travel 72 miles.

Share and Show

Write a multiplication or division sentence for each model.

1.

_____

2.
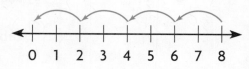

0 1 2 3 4 5 6 7 8

_____

8

Name _____

Draw a quick picture to find the product or quotient.

3. $25 \div 5 = $ _____

4. $18 \div 2 = $ _____

✓ **5.** $10 \times 3 = $ _____

6. $8 \times 7 = $ _____

7. $8 \times 2 = $ _____

✓ **8.** $32 \div 4 = $ _____

Math Talk Describe two different ways to model $45 \div 5$.

On Your Own

Draw a quick picture to find the product or quotient.

9. $6 \times 5 = $ _____

10.
$$\begin{array}{r} 3 \\ \times\ 9 \\ \hline \end{array}$$

11. $49 \div 7 = $ _____

Practice: Copy and Solve Draw a quick picture to find the product or quotient.

12. $1\overline{)9}$

13.
$$\begin{array}{r} 0 \\ \times\ 6 \\ \hline \end{array}$$

14.
$$\begin{array}{r} 3 \\ \times\ 8 \\ \hline \end{array}$$

15. $3\overline{)18}$

16. 9×9

17. $10 \div 2$

18. 6×4

19. $9 \div 9$

20. $20 \div 4$

GO DEEPER **Algebra** **Find the unknown number.**

21. $7 \times 6 = $ ■

■ $= $ _____

22. ■ $\div 8 = 6$

■ $= $ _____

23. $70 \div $ ■ $= 7$

■ $= $ _____

24. $9 \times $ ■ $= 45$

■ $= $ _____

Problem Solving • Applications

Use the menu for 25–27.

25. Ben bought 2 barbecue beef sandwiches and a drink. How much change did he get from a $20 bill?

_____

26. How much will it cost to buy 3 pieces of barbecue chicken, 1 barbecue beef sandwich, and 4 drinks?

_____

Bob's Barbecue Stand Menu

Barbecue beef sandwich $5

Piece of barbecue chicken $4

Bag of chips $1

All drinks $2

27. **GO DEEPER** **What's the Question?** The answer to a multiplication sentence is $45.

_____

_____

WRITE _Math_ • **Show Your Work**

28. **Pose a Problem** Write a word problem that can be solved by using the number line.

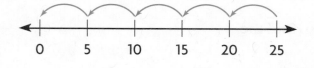

_____

_____

_____

29. **THINK SMARTER** Ellie divided 60 strawberries evenly among 10 classmates. How many strawberries did each classmate get?

(A) 5

(C) 8

(B) 6

(D) 10

Model Equal Groups

Learning Objective You will use models to solve multiplication and division problems.

Draw a quick picture to find the product or quotient.

1. $5 \times 4 =$ ___20___

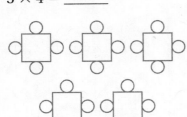

2. $21 \div 3 =$ ___7___

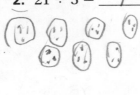

3. $\begin{array}{r} 2 \\ \times\ 7 \\ \hline \end{array}$

4. $28 \div 7 =$ _____

5. $\begin{array}{r} 7 \\ \times\ 5 \\ \hline \end{array}$

6. $8 \times 0 =$ _____

7. $6 \div 1 =$ _____

8. $18 \div 3 =$ _____

9. $10 \times 4 =$ _____

Problem Solving Real World

10. Isaiah has 8 goody bags for his party. He puts 5 party favors in each bag. How many party favors are there in all?

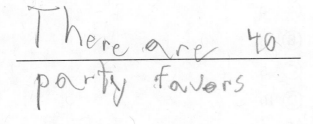

There are 40 party favors

11. There are 36 swings in all at the park. Each swing set has 6 swings on it. How many swing sets are there at the park?

_____

Lesson Check

1. Which problem is represented by the model below?

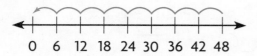

$$0 \quad 6 \quad 12 \quad 18 \quad 24 \quad 30 \quad 36 \quad 42 \quad 48$$

Ⓐ $6 \times 8 = 48$

Ⓑ $48 - 6 = 42$

Ⓒ $48 \div 6 = 8$

Ⓓ $48 - 42 = 6$

2. Hon places 4 pickle slices on each of 6 hamburgers. How many pickle slices does Hon use in all?

Ⓐ 6

Ⓑ 12

Ⓒ 18

Ⓓ 24

Spiral Review

3. Write four hundred three thousand, one hundred seventeen in standard form.

403,117

_____

4. Write 327,641 in expanded form.

300,000 + 20,000 + 7,000 + 600 + 40 + 1

_____

5. Mike has 48 toy cars. He buys 15 more toy cars. How many toy cars does Mike have?

Ⓐ 63

Ⓑ 33

Ⓒ 27

Ⓓ 18

6. Devon has 15 fruit snacks. He gives 5 to Debbie and 5 to Larry. How many fruit snacks does Devon have left to give to Brandon?

Ⓐ 0

Ⓑ 3

Ⓒ 5

Ⓓ 10

Name _____

Model Arrays and Area Models

Essential Question How can you model multiplication and division problems by using arrays and area models?

Learning Objective You will use arrays and area models to model multiplication and division problems.

🔑 Unlock the Problem (Real World)

🔑 One Way Make an array.

A A booth at the Florida State Fair in Tampa has 15 pies. There are 3 rows of pies, with the same number of pies in each row. How many pies are there in each row?

COMPLETE THE MODEL

THINK

_____ pies in all

_____ rows of pies

_____ pies in each row

RECORD

$$15 \div 3 = 5 \text{ or } 3\overline{)15}^{\,5}$$

↑   ↑   ↑
dividend divisor quotient

So, there are 5 pies in each row.

B A booth at the fair has pies in 3 rows, with 5 pies in each row. How many pies are there in all?

COMPLETE THE MODEL

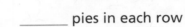

THINK

_____ rows

_____ pies in each row

_____ pies in all

RECORD

$$\begin{array}{r} 5 \leftarrow \text{factor} \\ \times\, 3 \leftarrow \text{factor} \\ \hline 15 \leftarrow \text{product} \end{array}$$

So, the booth has 15 pies.

Try This! **What if** there are 5 rows, with 3 pies in each row? How many pies are there in all?

COMPLETE THE MODEL	THINK	RECORD
Draw an array.	_____ rows _____ pies in each row _____ pies in all	

So, there are _____ pies in all.

❶ Another Way Make an area model.

A The fair has a treasure hunt map. The map is 10 squares long and 5 squares wide. How many squares are in the map?

MODEL	THINK	RECORD
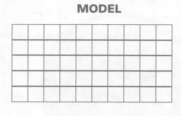	_____ squares long _____ squares wide _____ squares in all	10 ← factor × 5 ← factor ———— 50 ← product

So, the map has 50 squares in all.

B The fair has a treasure hunt map that covers 50 squares. The map is 10 squares long. How many squares wide is the map?

MODEL	THINK	RECORD
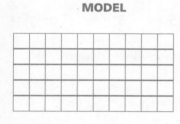	_____ squares in all _____ squares long _____ squares wide	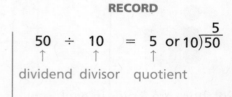

In the RECORD section:

$$50 \div 10 = 5 \text{ or } 10\overline{)50}^{\,5}$$

↑ dividend   ↑ divisor   ↑ quotient

So, the map is 10 squares wide.

Try This! **What if** the map covers 50 squares and is 5 squares wide? How many squares long is the map?

MODEL	THINK	RECORD
Draw an area model.	_____ squares in all _____ squares wide _____ squares long	_____

So, the map is _____ squares long.

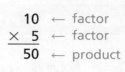 **Math Talk** When can you use division to solve a problem?

Name _____

1. Write the multiplication sentences
   these arrays show.

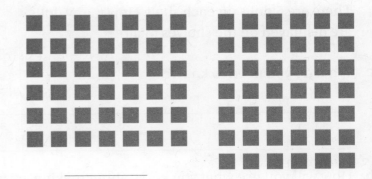

_____

_____

Draw a quick picture to find the product or quotient.

2. _____ = 24 ÷ 4   ✓ 3. $9 \times 9 =$ _____   ✓ 4. $14 \div 7 =$ _____

Math Talk Describe two different
ways to model 60 ÷ 10.

On Your Own

Draw a quick picture to find the product or quotient.

5. $7 \times 5 =$ _____   6. $27 \div 9 =$ _____   7. _____ $= 9 \times 2$

Practice: Copy and Solve Draw a quick picture to find the
product or quotient.

8. 5×5 9. $28 \div 7$ 10. $3)\overline{18}$ 11. 8×7

12. $2)\overline{16}$ 13. $\begin{array}{r} 9 \\ \times\ 4 \\ \hline \end{array}$ 14. $\begin{array}{r} 2 \\ \times\ 7 \\ \hline \end{array}$ 15. $10 \div 10$

GO DEEPER Write <, >, or = .

16. $16 \div 4 \bigcirc 2 \times 2$ 17. $10 \times 2 \bigcirc 20 \div 2$ 18. $45 \div 5 \bigcirc 6 \times 3$

Unlock the Problem

19. Madison displays her miniature dolls on 6 shelves. There are 5 dolls on each shelf. How many dolls are displayed on the shelves in all?

a. What do you need to know?

_____

_____

b. How will you use what you know about making arrays and area models to solve the problem?

_____

_____

c. What operation would you use to solve the problem?

_____

d. Draw an array or area model to find how many dolls are on all the shelves.

e. Complete the sentences.

Madison's dolls are displayed on

_____ shelves.

Madison has _____ dolls on each shelf.

Madison has _____ dolls on the shelves in all.

20. Tad put his baseball cards in 10 rows. Each row has 8 cards in it. How many baseball cards in all does Tad have?

_____

21. THINK SMARTER   Dave had 24 apples. He divided them equally among 4 of his friends. How many apples does each of his friends have?

(A) 28

(B) 24

(C) 6

(D) 4

Name _____

Model Arrays and Area Models

Learning Objective You will use arrays and area models to model multiplication and division problems.

Draw a quick picture to find the product or quotient.

1. $24 \div 4 =$ ___6___

2. $8 \times 9 =$ _____

3. $5\overline{)30}$

4. $\begin{array}{r} 7 \\ \times\ 7 \\ \hline \end{array}$

5. $4 \div 4 =$ _____

6. $10 \times 10 =$ _____

7. $42 \div 7 =$ _____

8. $\begin{array}{r} 3 \\ \times\ 0 \\ \hline \end{array}$

9. $40 \div 5 =$ _____

Problem Solving Real World

10. One page of Jenna's baseball card album holds 25 cards. There are 5 cards in each row. How many rows of cards are there?

11. Louisa knits a doll scarf with stripes. For each color stripe, she knits 8 rows of 8 stitches. How many total stitches are in each color stripe?

_____

_____

Lesson Check

1. Carly places 10 books on each of 4 shelves in her bedroom. How many books in all are on the shelves?

   (A) 44   (C) 20

   (B) 40   (D) 14

2. Tyrone draws a map of his neighborhood that covers 35 square blocks. The map is 5 blocks wide. How many blocks long is the map?

   (A) 5   (C) 7

   (B) 6   (D) 8

Spiral Review

3. Reese made a design for her mom using 36 tiles. She used 6 tiles in each row. How many rows of tiles does the design have?

   (A) 3

   (B) 6

   (C) 12

   (D) 18

4. Which number has a 5 in the ten thousands place?

   (A) 363,754

   (B) 587,902

   (C) 652,806

   (D) 765,327

5. Write a multiplication sentence that represents the given array.

   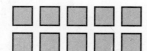

   _____

6. A web page had over 906,000 visitors. Write the number of visitors in word form.

   _____

Name _____

Relate Multiplication and Division

Essential Question How can you write a set of related multiplication and division facts?

Unlock the Problem

Multiplication and division by the same number are opposite operations, or **inverse operations**. One operation undoes the other.

How can you use inverse operations to solve a problem?

🔑 **Use related multiplication and division sentences.**

Ⓐ A group of 16 people are going on a train ride at the zoo. Each car holds 2 people. How many cars will they need?

$16 \div 2 = $ ■   Think: $8 \times 2 = 16$, so $16 \div 2 = $ _____.
      ↓
$16 \div 2 = 8$

So, _____ train cars will be needed.

Ⓑ Another train has 2 cars. Each car can hold 8 people. How many people can ride the train at one time?

$2 \times 8 = $ ■   Think: $16 \div 2 = 8$, so $2 \times 8 = $ _____.
      ↓
$2 \times 8 = 16$

So, _____ people can ride the train at one time.

- Circle what you are asked to find.
- Underline the information you will use.

Math Talk Opening and closing a door are inverse actions. What are some other examples of inverses?

Related facts are a set of multiplication and division sentences that are related.

		Related Facts			
factor	factor	product	dividend	divisor	quotient
2 ×	8 =	16	16 ÷	2 =	_____.
8 ×	2 =	_____.	16 ÷	8 =	_____.

- Why do some sets of related facts have only two number sentences in them? Give an example.

Use Inverse Operations Carla's class used models to show that multiplication and division are inverse operations. This is how the students explained and showed their work.

🔑 Example 1 Use a factor triangle card.

Ella used 21 rectangles to make some quilt blocks for a rail fence quilt. How many quilt blocks did she make?

Since Ella used 21 rectangles, I used the factor triangle card for the product 21 and the factor 3 to find the unknown factor, 7. The unknown factor is the quotient.

$21 \div 3 = 7$, so _____ $\times$ 3 = _____.

▲ In a rail fence quilt, each quilt block is made by sewing 3 rectangular strips of fabric together.

🔑 Example 2 Use a number line.

Jon's quilt is 2 times as long as Mia's quilt. Mia's quilt is 4 blocks long. How long is Jon's quilt?

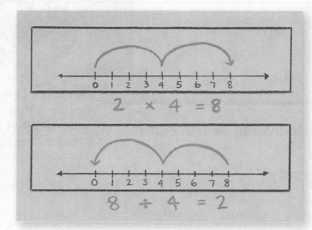

I started at 0 on a number line and made 2 jumps of 4 to land at 8. Then to check I used the inverse operation. I started at 8 and

took _____ jumps of _____ back to 0.

Name _____

Find the product or quotient. Then write a related multiplication or division sentence.

1. $2 \times 5 =$ _____

2. $6 \div 2 =$ _____

3. $2 \times 4 =$ _____

_____

Write the related multiplication and division sentences to complete the set of related facts.

4. $3 \times 6 = 18$

5. $12 \div 3 = 4$

6. $6 \times 2 = 12$

_____

_____

Math Talk Explain why division by a number is the inverse of multiplication by that number. Give an example. You may wish to draw a model.

On Your Own

Write the related multiplication and division sentences to complete the set of related facts.

7. $14 \div 7 = 2$

8. $1 \times 4 = 4$

9. $9 \div 3 = 3$

_____

_____

Find the product or quotient.

10. $6 \times 2 =$ _____

11. _____ $= 9 \div 1$

12. $9 \times 3 =$ _____

13. $28 \div 4 =$ _____

14. _____ $= 4 \times 1$

15. $8 \times 5 =$ _____

16. $24 \div 4 =$ _____

17. _____ $= 8 \times 4$

GO DEEPER **Algebra** Find the unknown number. Then write a related multiplication or division sentence.

18. ■ $\times 3 = 27$

19. $8 \div$ ■ $= 8$

20. $36 \div$ ■ $= 9$

21. ■ $\times 4 = 28$

■ $=$ _____

■ $=$ _____

■ $=$ _____

■ $=$ _____

_____

Problem Solving • Applications Real World

Use the picture graph for 22–23.

22. **GO DEEPER** How many different shades of crayon colors does the crayon factory make?

_____

23. **What if** the crayon factory made 8 different shades of yellow? How many symbols would represent 8 shades in the picture graph?

_____

24. The average American child will use up about 730 crayons by the age of 10, or about 6 crayons each month. About how many crayons will a child use up in 4 months?

_____

25. **GO DEEPER** **What's the Error?** Dale says that 6×2 is in the same set of related facts as $6 \div 2$. **Explain** his error.

_____

_____

_____

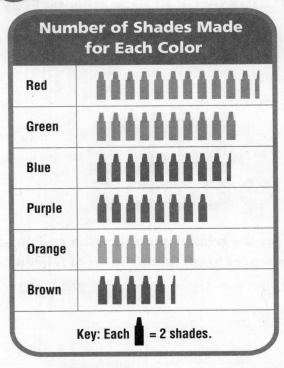

Number of Shades Made for Each Color

Red	
Green	
Blue	
Purple	
Orange	
Brown	

Key: Each █ = 2 shades.

• • • • • • • • • **WRITE** ▸ *Math* • **Show Your Work** • • • •

26. **THINK SMARTER** Ally colored 3 pages in a coloring book. Becca colored 6 times as many pages as Ally colored. Which of the following could you use to find the number of pages Becca colored?

(A) 6×3 (C) $6 - 3$

(B) $6 + 3$ (D) $6 \div 3$

Name _____

Relate Multiplication and Division

Learning Objective You will use inverse operations and related facts to solve for products and quotients.

Write the related multiplication and division sentences to complete the set of related facts.

1. $3 \times 6 = 18$

     $6 \times 3 = 18$

     $18 \div 6 = 3$

     $18 \div 3 = 6$

2. $28 \div 4 = 7$

_____

_____

_____

3. $9 \div 9 = 1$

_____

_____

_____

4. $8 \times 2 = 16$

_____

_____

_____

5. $20 \div 4 = 5$

_____

_____

_____

6. $3 \times 9 = 27$

_____

_____

_____

Find the product or quotient.

7. $7 \times 2 =$ _____

8. $24 \div 3 =$ _____

9. _____ $= 16 \div 4$

10. $3 \times 1 =$ _____

11. $36 \div 4 =$ _____

12. _____ $= 7 \div 7$

13. $5 \times 6 =$ _____

14. _____ $= 4 \times 2$

Problem Solving

Use the graph for 15–16.

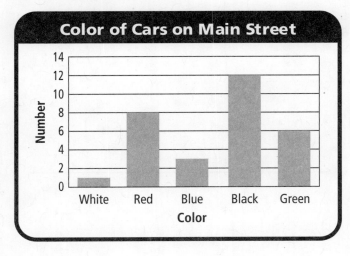

15. There are 8 times as many red cars as white cars. Write a multiplication problem to show this.

_____

16. There are 4 times as many of which color car as there are blue cars on Main Street?

_____

Lesson Check

1. Which of the following is the set of related facts for the numbers 5, 8, and 40?

   Ⓐ $5 \times 40 = 8$, $8 \times 40 = 5$, $40 \div 8 = 5$, $40 \div 5 = 8$

   Ⓑ $5 \times 8 = 40$, $8 \times 5 = 40$, $8 - 5 = 3$, $40 - 8 = 32$

   Ⓒ $5 \times 8 = 40$, $8 \times 5 = 40$, $40 \div 8 = 5$, $40 \div 5 = 8$

   Ⓓ $5 \times 40 = 200$, $40 \times 5 = 200$, $40 - 5 = 35$, $40 - 8 = 32$

2. Tess made the following array to find the product 3×7.

   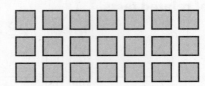

   She can use the array to find the quotient $21 \div 3$. What is the quotient?

   Ⓐ 3

   Ⓑ 7

   Ⓒ 9

   Ⓓ 21

Spiral Review

3. Which number is represented by point C in the number line below?

   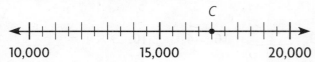

   Ⓐ 17,000

   Ⓑ 16,500

   Ⓒ 16,000

   Ⓓ 15,500

4. Between which two numbers is 48,603?

   Ⓐ 47,000 and 48,000

   Ⓑ 47,500 and 48,500

   Ⓒ 48,000 and 49,000

   Ⓓ 49,000 and 50,000

5. Write seven hundred forty-six thousand, three hundred two in standard form.

   _____

6. Write 707,312 in expanded form.

   _____

Name _____

Use Multiplication and Division Strategies

Essential Question How can you use strategies to help you recall multiplication and division facts?

Learning Objective You will use different strategies to recall multiplication and division facts.

🔑 Unlock the Problem

Using strategies can help you learn the multiplication and division facts that you do not know.

Roger has a block puzzle that has 6 rows, with 7 blocks in each row. How many blocks are in Roger's puzzle?

🔑 Activity Use the break apart strategy.

Materials ■ centimeter grid paper ■ scissors

To find the product of 6 and 7, you can break apart one of the factors into products you know.

STEP 1 Draw a rectangle with 6 rows of 7 units.

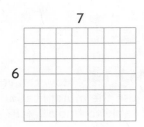

STEP 2 Cut apart the model to make two smaller rectangles for products you know.

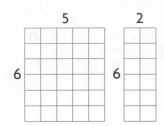

The factor 7 is broken into _____ plus _____.

STEP 3 Find the sum of the products of the two smaller rectangles.

6 × _____ = 30

6 × _____ = 12

_____ + _____ = _____

So, there are 42 blocks in Roger's puzzle.

Try This! **What if** you cut apart the model horizontally?
Show other ways you can break apart the 6 × 7 model.

🔑 Examples

A Use a multiplication table.

Find 5 × 7.

- Shade the row for the factor 5.
- Shade the column for the factor 7.
- Look down column 7. The product is found where row 5 and column 7 meet. Circle the product.

×	0	1	2	3	4	5	6	7	8	9	10
0	0	0	0	0	0	0	0	0	0	0	0
1	0	1	2	3	4	5	6	7	8	9	10
2	0	2	4	6	8	10	12	14	16	18	20
3	0	3	6	9	12	15	18	21	24	27	30
4	0	4	8	12	16	20	24	28	32	36	40
5	0	5	10	15	20	25	30	35	40	45	50
6	0	6	12	18	24	30	36	42	48	54	60
7	0	7	14	21	28	35	42	49	56	63	70
8	0	8	16	24	32	40	48	56	64	72	80
9	0	9	18	27	36	45	54	63	72	81	90
10	0	10	20	30	40	50	60	70	80	90	100

So, $5 \times 7 = 35$.

Math Talk How can you use the multiplication table to find $56 \div 8$?

B Use doubles.
Multiply. 10 × 5

Think: The factor 10 is an even number.
$5 + 5 = 10$

_____ $\times 5 = 25$

_____ $\times 5 = 25$

$25 + 25 =$ _____

So, $5 \times 10 =$ _____.

C Use the Commutative Property.
Multiply. 4 × 8

If you know 8×4, use that fact to find 4×8.

$8 \times 4 =$ _____.

So, $4 \times 8 =$ _____.

D Use inverse operations.
Divide. 63 ÷ 9

Think: $9 \times 7 = 63$

So, $63 \div 9 =$ _____.

Name _____

1. Use the models to complete the sentences.

$6 \times 5 =$ _____

$6 \times 4 =$ _____

$6 \times 9 =$ _____ + _____

So, $6 \times 9 =$ _____.

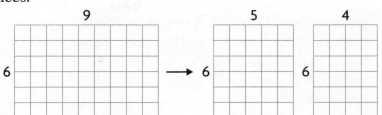

Find the product or quotient. Write the strategy you used. Write
model, break apart, multiplication table, inverse operations,
pattern, **or** *doubles.*

2. $8 \times 6 =$ _____

3. $63 \div 7 =$ _____

✔ **4.** _____ $= 5 \times 8$

✔ **5.** $14 \div 7 =$ _____

Math Talk Describe two strategies you can use to find 8×7.

On Your Own

Find the product or quotient. Write the strategy you used.
Write *model, break apart, multiplication table, inverse operations,*
pattern, **or** *doubles.*

6. $3 \times 6 =$ _____

7. $49 \div 7 =$ _____

8. _____ $= 3 \times 9$

9. _____ $= 9 \div 9$

10. $6\overline{)12}$

11. 10
     $\times\ 5$

12. 8
     $\times\ 1$

13. $8\overline{)24}$

GO DEEPER **Algebra** Find the value of the coins.

14.

Dimes	1	2	4	6	8
Cents	10				

15.

Nickels	5	6	7	8	9
Cents	25				

Problem Solving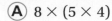

**Use the Checkers Marathon Game 1
Results for 16–18.**

Checkers Marathon

Game 1 Results

ED   TANYA   JAMAL

16. In the game of checkers, a king is 2 checkers
    stacked. Tanya has 3 kings. How many single
    checkers does she have?

    _____

17. What is the greatest number of kings that Jamal
    could have?

    _____

18. Ed had the same number of checkers left at
    the end of each game. He ended the checkers
    marathon with a total of 45 checkers left. How
    many games did Ed play?

    _____

· · · · · · · · **WRITE** ▸*Math* · **Show Your Work** · · · ·

19. **GO DEEPER** **WRITE** ▸*Math* Find the unknown
    numbers. Describe the relationships between
    the products. **Explain** why the products have
    these relationships.

    $6 \times 2 =$ _____

    $6 \times 4 =$ _____

    $6 \times 8 =$ _____

    $6 \times 16 =$ _____

    _____

    _____

    _____

20. **THINK SMARTER** Gertrude drew rectangles
    on grid paper to find the product 8×9. Which
    of the following describes Gertrude's drawing?

    (A) $8 \times (5 \times 4)$ (C) $(8 + 5) + (8 + 4)$

    (B) $8 + 9$ (D) $(8 \times 5) + (8 \times 4)$

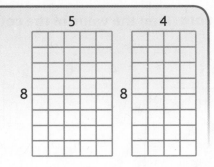

Use Multiplication and Division Strategies

Learning Objective You will use different strategies to recall multiplication and division facts.

Find the product or quotient. Write the strategy you used.
Write *model*, *break apart*, *multiplication table*, *inverse operations*, *pattern*, or *doubles*.

1. $9 \times 6 =$ ___54___

2. $56 \div 7 =$ _____

3. $7\overline{)42}$

4. _____ $= 9 \times 9$

doubles
$6 = 3 + 3$
$9 \times 3 = 27$
$9 \times 3 = 27$
$27 + 27 = 54$

5. _____ $= 36 \div 9$

6. $7\overline{)49}$

7. $40 \div 10 =$ _____

8. _____ $= 3 \times 6$

9. 8
      $\times\ 4$

10. 0
       $\times\ 7$

11. _____ $= 8 \times 6$

12. $9\overline{)9}$

Problem Solving Real World

13. Randy has a piece of rope that is 36 feet long. He wants to cut it into 6 equal pieces to make jump ropes for his friends. How long will each rope be?

_____

14. Bailey buys 7 sheets of stickers. Each sheet has 2 rows of stickers with 3 stickers in each row. How many stickers does Bailey buy in all?

_____

Lesson Check

1. Which of the following is represented by the model?

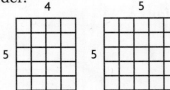

- (A) 5 + 9
- (B) 5 × (4 × 5)
- (C) (5 + 4) × (5 + 5)
- (D) (5 × 4) + (5 × 5)

2. Molly uses the doubles strategy to find the product 8 × 7. Which of the following could Molly use to find the product?

- (A) 4 + 4 + 7
- (B) (4 × 7) + (4 × 7)
- (C) (4 × 7) + 7
- (D) (4 × 7) + (4 + 7)

Spiral Review

3. Round 436,981 to the nearest ten thousand.

_____

4. Elliot wants to round the number 875,369 to the nearest hundred thousand. Which digit should he use to determine how to round?

- (A) 3
- (B) 5
- (C) 7
- (D) 9

5. Two tiles on the cafeteria wall have a star design on them as shown below.

Which can be used to find the total number of stars on the tiles?

- (A) 2 × 2
- (B) 2 × 9
- (C) 2 + 2
- (D) 2 + 9

6. Kayla bakes 24 cupcakes. She can bake 8 cupcakes in each batch. How many batches of cupcakes will Kayla make?

_____

Name _____

Multiplication Table Through 10

Essential Question How can you use a multiplication table to find products and quotients?

Learning Objective You will use a multiplication table to find products and quotients.

 Unlock the Problem *Real World*

You can use patterns and strategies to help you complete a multiplication table for the facts from 0 through 10.

Complete the multiplication table.

×	0	1	2	3	4	5	6	7	8	9	10
0											
1											
2											
3											
4											
5											
6											
7											
8											
9											
10											

Remember

The Zero Property of Multiplication states that the product of 0 and any number is 0.

The Identity Property of Multiplication states that the product of 1 and any number is that number.

Math Talk Describe the strategy you could use to find the product of 12 and 3.

- Use the Zero Property of Multiplication to complete the row and column for 0. Use the Identity Property of Multiplication to complete the row and column for 1.

- Use doubles to complete the row and column for 2.

- Count by fives to complete the row and column for 5.

- Count by nines to complete the row and column for 9.

- Now complete the rest of the table.

Example Use a multiplication table.

Divide. $48 \div 8 = $ ■

You can also use a multiplication table
to find the quotient in a division problem.

Think: $8 \times $ ■ $= 48$

STEP 1
  Complete the row for the given factor, 8.
  _____

STEP 2
  Look across to find the product, 48.
  _____

STEP 3
  Look up to find the unknown factor, _____.

So, $48 \div 8 = 6$.
In Step 1, is the divisor or the dividend the given
factor in the related multiplication fact?

_____

In Step 2, is the divisor or the dividend the
product?

_____

The quotient is the unknown factor.

×	0	1	2	3	4	5	6	7	8	9	10
0	0	0	0	0	0	0	0	0	0	0	0
1	0	1	2	3	4	5	6	7	8	9	10
2	0	2	4	6	8	10	12	14	16	18	20
3	0	3	6	9	12	15	18	21	24	27	30
4	0	4	8	12	16	20	24	28	32	36	40
5	0	5	10	15	20	25	30	35	40	45	50
6	0	6	12	18	24	30	36	42	48	54	60
7	0	7	14	21	28	35	42	49	56	63	70
8											
9	0	9	18	27	36	45	54	63	72	81	90
10	0	10	20	30	40	50	60	70	80	90	100

Math Talk Use the multiplication table
to show that $0 \div 5 = 0$. Then use the
table to show that $5 \div 0 = $ ■ does
not make sense.

Share and Show MATH BOARD

1. Use the related multiplication fact, $7 \times 10 = 70$, to find $70 \div 7$.

  _____

Find the product or quotient.

2. _____ $= 6 \times 3$

3. $56 \div 7 = $ _____

4. $81 \div 9 = $ _____

5. $100 \div 10 = $ _____

6. $8 \times 5 = $ _____

7. $5 \times 7 = $ _____

Math Talk Explain the difference
between 3×4 and 4×3 when finding
the product using a multiplication table.

Name _____

On Your Own

Find the product or quotient.

8. $\begin{array}{r} 6 \\ \times\ 8 \\ \hline \end{array}$

9. $8\overline{)64}$

10. $\begin{array}{r} 10 \\ \times\ 2 \\ \hline \end{array}$

11. _____ $= 10 \times 0$

12. $18 \div 9 =$ _____

13. $6 \times 9 =$ _____

14. $7 \times 6 =$ _____

15. _____ $= 5 \times 8$

16. $45 \div 5 =$ _____

17. $\begin{array}{r} 3 \\ \times\ 0 \\ \hline \end{array}$

18. $90 \div 9 =$ _____

19. _____ $= 18 \div 3$

GO DEEPER **Algebra** Use the rule to find the unknown numbers.

20. Rule: Multiply the input by 9.

Input	Output
1	
7	
8	
9	

21. Rule: Divide the input by 4.

Input	Output
8	
16	
24	
	8

22. Rule: Multiply the input by 10.

Input	Output
2	
	40
6	
	80

Problem Solving • Applications *Real World*

23. **WRITE** *Math* What could be the unknown factors in ★ × ▲ = 24? Find as many factor pairs as you can. **Explain** how you found these factors.

_____

_____

_____

_____

24. **THINK SMARTER** Susie has 5 bags, with 7 marbles in each bag. How many marbles does Susie have in all?

Ⓐ 5

Ⓑ 7

Ⓒ 35

Ⓓ 57

Sense or Nonsense?

25. Whose statement makes sense? Whose statement is nonsense?
Explain your reasoning.

The column for 3 and the row for 3 in the multiplication table show the same products.

You can add 1 to each product in the column for 4 to find the products for 5 in the column for 5.

Chad

Rachael

• For the statement that is nonsense, write a new statement that makes sense.

Multiplication Table
Through 10

Learning Objective You will use a multiplication table to find products and quotients.

Find the product or quotient.

1. $72 \div 8 =$ ___9___

2.   7
       $\times\ \underline{6}$

3. $40 \div 10 =$ _____

4. $6 \times 4 =$ _____

5. $9\overline{)63}$

6. _____ $= 5 \times 10$

7. $36 \div 6 =$ _____

8.   9
       $\times\ \underline{4}$

9. $7 \times 7 =$ _____

10. $8\overline{)56}$

11. $8 \times 10 =$ _____

12. _____ $= 54 \div 6$

Problem Solving Real World

Use the multiplication table for 13–14.

×	0	1	2	3	4	5	6	7	8	9	10
0	0	0	0	0	0	0	0	0	0	0	0
1	0	1	2	3	4	5	6	7	8	9	10
2	0	2	4	6	8	10	12	14	16	18	20
3	0	3	6	9	12	15	18	21	24	27	30
4	0	4	8	12	16	20	24	28	32	36	40
5	0	5	10	15	20	25	30	35	40	45	50
6	0	6	12	18	24	30	36	42	48	54	60
7	0	7	14	21	28	35	42	49	56	63	70
8	0	8	16	24	32	40	48	56	64	72	80
9	0	9	18	27	36	45	54	63	72	81	90
10	0	10	20	30	40	50	60	70	80	90	100

13. Jon says the products in the column for 10 are twice the products in the column for 5. Kate says the products in the column for 10 are five more than the products in the column for 5. Who is correct?

_____

14. In which two columns and rows can you find the product 63?

_____

_____

_____

Lesson Check

1. Benji looked down the column for 10 in a multiplication table and found the product 60. In which row of the table would the product that Benji found be located?

   (A) row for the factor 6

   (B) row for the factor 7

   (C) row for the factor 8

   (D) row for the factor 9

2. In which column of a multiplication table is every product the same?

   (A) column for the factor 9

   (B) column for the factor 5

   (C) column for the factor 1

   (D) column for the factor 0

Spiral Review

3. Which number is three hundred eight thousand, four hundred sixty-eight written in standard form?

   (A) 380,468

   (B) 308,468

   (C) 38,846

   (D) 3,848

4. Sabrina is thinking of an 3-digit number. The digit in the hundreds place is three times the digit in the ones place. The digit in the ones place is three more than the digit in the tens place. Which of the following could be Sabrina's number?

   (A) 341

   (B) 652

   (C) 903

   (D) 913

5. Jared had $13,900 in his savings account. The car he wants to buy cost $18,450. How much more money does Jared need to save to be able to buy the car?

6. At the start of a football game, there were 24,439 people sitting in the stands. By the end of the third quarter, there were only 17,389 people sitting in the stands. How many people left the stands by the end of the third quarter?

Name _____

Multiplication Properties

Essential Question How can you use multiplication properties to help you solve problems mentally?

Learning Objective You will use mental math and multiplication properties to find products.

 Unlock the Problem

How can you use the properties of multiplication to help you find products of two or more factors?

Zero Property of Multiplication

The product of 0 and any number is 0.

3 groups of 0 fish

3 × 0 = _____

Identity Property of Multiplication

The product of 1 and any number is that number.

1 group of 3 fish

1 × 3 = _____

Commutative Property of Multiplication

You can multiply two factors in any order and get the same product.

2 rows of 3 birds   3 rows of 2 birds

2 × 3 = _____   3 × 2 = _____

Associative Property of Multiplication

You can group factors in different ways and get the same product. Use parentheses ( ) to group the factors you multiply first.

4 groups of 2 dog   4 times 2 groups of
biscuits, 3 times   3 dog biscuits

(4 × 2) × 3 = _____   4 × (2 × 3) = _____

- Use counters to show two ways you can group 3 × 2 × 4 to find the product. Are the products the same? Explain.

_____

_____

 Draw a picture to show what you did.

🔑 Activity 1 Use the Distributive Property.

Materials ■ square tiles

The **Distributive Property** states that multiplying a sum by a number is the same as multiplying each addend by the number and then adding the products.

Multiply. 4×8

STEP 1

Make a model to find 4×8. Use square tiles to build an array.

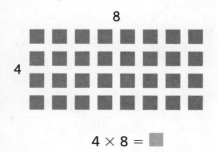

$4 \times 8 = $ ■

So, $4 \times 8 = 32$.

STEP 2

Break apart the array to make two smaller arrays for products you know.

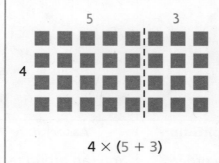

$4 \times (5 + 3)$

STEP 3

Use the Distributive Property to show the sum of the two products.

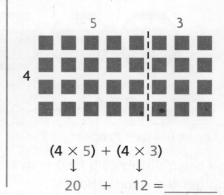

$(4 \times 5) + (4 \times 3)$
↓ ↓
$20 \ + \ 12 = $ _____

> **Math Talk** Restate in your own words the definition of the Distributive Property.

🔑 Example 1 Use the properties to find the unknown factor.

Ⓐ

■ $\times 8 = 0$

☐ $\times 8 = 0$ Zero Property

■ $= 0$

Ⓑ

$7 \times$ ■ $= 6 \times 7$

$7 \times$ ☐ $= 6 \times 7$ Commutative Property

■ $= 6$

🔑 Example 2 Use the properties and mental math to find the product.

Find $3 \times 10 \times 2$.

$3 \times 10 \times 2 = 3 \times 2 \times 10$ Commutative Property

$\quad\quad\quad = (3 \times 2) \times 10$ Associative Property

$\quad\quad\quad = $ _____ $\times$ _____

$\quad\quad\quad = $ _____

> **Math Talk** Is $27 \times (48 - 48) = 0$ true? **Explain** how you can easily see this.

Name _____

1. Use the Associative Property to find the unknown factor.

   $(3 \times) \times 6 = 3 \times (2 \times 6)$

Use the properties and mental math to find the product.

2. $1 \times 9 \times 1$ 3. $24 \times 0 \times 6$ ✓ 4. $10 \times 5 \times 2$ ✓ 5. 4×7

_____   _____   _____   _____

Math Talk Explain how the Commutative Property works for 4×8 and 8×4. Make a model or draw a picture.

On Your Own

Use the properties and mental math to find the product.

6. $9 \times 7 \times 0$ 7. $2 \times 4 \times 10$ 8. $5 \times 5 \times 4$ 9. $2 \times 3 \times 4$

_____   _____   _____   _____

Find the unknown number. Name the property used.

10. $8 \times 6 = 6 \times $ 11. $10 = 10 \times $ 12. $ = 0 \times 4$

_____   _____   _____

Show two ways to group by using parentheses. Find the product.

13. $3 \times 3 \times 10 =$ _____   14. $8 \times 7 \times 1 =$ _____   15. $7 \times 3 \times 2 =$ _____

_____   _____   _____

_____   _____   _____

GO DEEPER Draw a model and use the Distributive Property to find the product.

16. $13 \times 5 =$ _____   17. $9 \times 11 =$ _____   18. $6 \times 12 =$ _____

⚷ Unlock the Problem

19. A chef receives 2 boxes of egg cartons. Each box has 4 cartons of eggs. There are 6 eggs in each carton. How many eggs does the chef receive?

   Ⓐ 12   Ⓑ 24   Ⓒ 48   Ⓓ 72

a. What do you need to find? _____

_____

b. How can you use multiplication properties to find the number of eggs the chef receives?

_____

_____

c. How will you group the factors to find the number of eggs the chef receives?

_____

_____

d. Show how you can solve the problem.

e. Complete the sentences.

There are _____ boxes of egg cartons.

There are _____ egg cartons in each box.

There are _____ eggs in each carton.

The chef receives _____ eggs.

f. Fill in the bubble for the correct answer choice above.

20. John's school has 4 classrooms. Each classroom has 2 fishbowls. Each fishbowl has 5 fish. How many fish does John's school have?

   Ⓐ   8

   Ⓑ 10

   Ⓒ 11

   Ⓓ 40

21. **THINK SMARTER** Tilly has 8 boxes of baseball cards. Each box has 12 cards in it. The product of 8×12 represents the total number of baseball cards Tilly has.

Which of the following also represents how many baseball cards Tilly has?

   Ⓐ $8 \times 4 \times 8$ Ⓒ $(8 \times 4) + (8 \times 8)$

   Ⓑ $(8 \times 10) \times 2$ Ⓓ $(8 \times 1) + (8 \times 2)$

Name _____

Multiplication Properties

Learning Objective You will use mental math and multiplication properties to find products.

Use the properties and mental math to find the product.

1. $3 \times 6 \times 2$

$3 \times (6 \times 2) =$ _____

$3 \times (2 \times 6) =$ _____

$(3 \times 2) \times 6 =$ _____

$6 \times 6 =$ __36__ _____

2. $8 \times 6 \times 0$

_____

3. $2 \times 7 \times 4$

_____

Find the unknown number. Name the property used.

4. $6 \times \boxed{} = 6$

_____

5. $4 \times 7 = \boxed{} \times 4$

_____

6. $5 \times \boxed{} = 0$

_____

7. $(6 \times 4) \times 2 = \boxed{} \times (4 \times 2)$

_____

8. $5 \times 8 = (5 \times 4) + (\boxed{} \times 4)$

_____

Show two ways to group by using parentheses. Find the product.

9. $7 \times 1 \times 10 =$ _____

_____

_____

10. $8 \times 2 \times 5 =$ _____

_____

_____

11. $3 \times 7 \times 0 =$ _____

_____

_____

 Problem Solving Real World

12. Two teams of 9 children gather to play baseball. Each child brings 1 glove. How many gloves are there in all?

_____

13. Cedric, Lauren, and Jay each bought 4 packs of trading cards. Each pack costs $3. How much did the three friends spend on cards all together?

_____

Lesson Check

1. Which of the following represents the Commutative Property of Multiplication?

   (A) $5 \times (4 \times 3) = (5 \times 4) \times 3$

   (B) $5 \times 1 = 5$

   (C) $5 \times 7 = 7 \times 5$

   (D) $5 \times 9 = (5 \times 6) + (5 \times 3)$

2. Six friends meet to play a round of golf. Each brings 2 packs of golf balls. Each pack has 3 balls. How many golf balls do the friends have in all?

   (A) 11   (C) 18

   (B) 12   (D) 36

Spiral Review

3. What is another way to write $7 + 7 + 7 + 7 = 28$?

   _____

   _____

   _____

4. A museum has 39,435 visitors in one month. Write the number of visitors in expanded form.

   _____

   _____

   _____

5. Which shows the numbers in order from least to greatest?

   (A) 15,489; 14,832; 15,410

   (B) 14,832; 15,489; 15,410

   (C) 14,832; 15,410; 15,489

   (D) 15,489; 15,410; 14,832

6. Caleb buys 3 bunches of bananas. There are 5 bananas in each bunch. How many bananas are in 3 groups of 5 bananas?

   (A) 10

   (B) 15

   (C) 20

   (D) 25

Name _____

Describe Relationships

Essential Question How can you use equations and tables to represent functions?

You can use an input/output table to show a pattern. A pattern is called a **function** when one quantity depends on the other. You can write a rule, or equation, to describe the relationship between the inputs and outputs of a function.

Some functions can be represented by an equation with two variables, such as $y = x + 3$. For each input x, there is exactly one output y.

Learning Objective You will use equations to describe relationships between two variables.

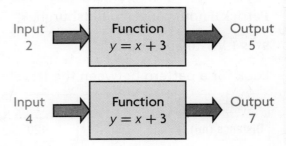

Input 2 → Function $y = x + 3$ → Output 5

Input 4 → Function $y = x + 3$ → Output 7

Unlock the Problem

A bowling alley charges $5 for each hour of bowling, plus $3 to rent shoes. Write an equation for the function that gives the total cost y in dollars for skating x hours. Then make a table that shows the cost of bowling for 1, 2, 3, and 4 hours.

Math Idea

There are several ways to show multiplication with a variable. Each expression below represents "3 times y."

$3 \times y$ $3y$ $3(y)$ $3 \cdot y$

🔑 **Write an equation for the function, and use the equation to make a table.**

STEP 1 Write an equation.

Think:

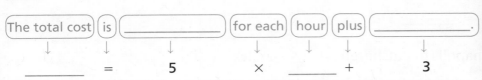

The total cost | is | _____ | for each | hour | plus | _____.

_____ = 5 × _____ + 3

So, the equation for the function is _____.

STEP 2 Make a table.

Input	Rule	Output
Time (h), x	$5x + 3$	Cost ($), y
1	$5 \times 1 + 3$	8
2		
3		
4		

Replace x in the function rule with each input value, then use the order of operations to find each output value.

Math Talk Explain how you could use the equation to find the total cost of bowling for 6 hours.

🔑 Example

Patrick drives his car from Indianapolis to Pittsburgh. The table shows how the distance he travels depends on how long he drives. Write an equation for the function shown in the table. Then use the equation to find the distance between Indianapolis and Pittsburgh if it takes Patrick 6 hours to get to Pittsburgh.

Travel Times	
Time (hr), x	Distance (mi), y
1	60
2	120
3	180
4	240
5	300

STEP 1 Write an equation.

Look for a pattern between the travel time and the distance.

Time (hr), x	1	2	3	4
Distance (mi), y	60	120	180	240

60×1 60×2 $60 \times$ _____ $60 \times$ _____

Think: You can find each distance by multiplying the travel time by _____.

Think: (The distance) (is) ( ) (multiplied by) (the travel time.)

_____ = 60 × _____

So, the equation for the function is _____.

_____

STEP 2 Use the equation to find the distance traveled in 6 hours.

Write the equation. $y = 60x$

Replace x with 6. $y = 60 \times$ _____

Solve for y. $y =$ _____

So, the distance from Indianapolis to Pittsburgh is _____ miles.

1. **Explain** how you can check that your equation for the function is correct.

_____

_____

2. **Describe** a situation in which it would be more useful to represent a function with an equation than with a table of values.

_____

_____

44

Name _____

Use the equation to complete the table.

1. $y = x + 3$

Input	Rule	Output
x	**x + 3**	**y**
1	1 + 3	
5	5 + 3	
13		

2. $y = 5x + 1$

Input	Output
x	**y**
4	
7	
10	

Write an equation for the function shown in the table. Then find the unknown value in the table.

3.

x	1	2	3	4
y	5	10		20

4.

x	5	10	15	20
y	0	5		15

_____

_____

> **Math Talk** **Explain** how to write an equation for a function shown by a table of values.

On Your Own

Write an equation for the function shown in the table. Then find the unknown value in the table.

5.

x	8	9	10	11
y	24	27		33

6.

x	4	8	16	32
y	2	4	8	

_____

7. **THINK SMARTER** It costs $13 to order a cheese pizza and $2 for each extra topping. Write an equation for the function that gives the total cost *y* in dollars for ordering a pizza with *x* extra toppings. Then complete the table.

Pizza Costs	
Extra Toppings, x	**Total cost ($), y**
3	
4	
5	

_____

Connect [to] Reading

Cause and Effect

The reading skill *cause and effect* can help you understand how a change in one variable may create a change in another variable.

An airline charges its passengers $25 for each bag they check. Tomas wants to check 3 bags on his trip. What effect will the number of bags have on his travel expenses?

Cause: Tomas checks 3 bags.	→	Effect: Tomas's travel expenses increase.

Write an equation for a function that relates the cause and effect. Then use the function to solve the problem.

Let *x* represent the number of bags Tomas checks, and let *y* represent the increase in dollars in his travel expenses.

Write the equation for the function. $y = \underline{\hspace{1cm}} \times x$ or $\underline{\hspace{1cm}} x$

Tomas wants to check 3 bags, so $y = 25 \times \underline{\hspace{1cm}}$

replace *x* with $\underline{\hspace{1cm}}$. $y = \underline{\hspace{1cm}}$
Solve for *y*.

So, if Tomas checks 3 bags on his trip, his travel expenses will increase by $\underline{\hspace{1cm}}$.

Write an equation for a function that relates the cause and effect. Then use the function to solve the problem.

8. Kayla flies with an airline that allows its passengers to check one free bag. The airline charges $40 for each additional bag. Kayla plans to check 2 bags. What effect will the number of bags have on her travel expenses?

9. An airline offers in-flight entertainment. It charges $1 per TV episode and sells headphones for an additional $2. What effect will the cost of in-flight entertainment have on Casey's travel expenses if he buys headphones and watches 9 TV episodes?

Describe Relationships

Learning Objective You will use equations to describe relationships between two variables.

Use the equation to complete the table.

1. $y = 6x$

Input	Output
x	y
2	12
5	30
8	48

2. $y = x - 7$

Input	Output
x	y
7	
10	
13	

3. $y = 3x + 1$

Input	Output
x	y
3	
4	
5	

Write an equation for the function shown in the table. Then find the unknown value in the table.

4.

x	2	3	4	5
y	18	27	36	■

5.

x	7	8	9	10
y	49	■	63	70

_____

6.

x	2	4	6	8
y	■	2	4	6

7.

x	0	3	6	9
y	4	10	■	22

_____

 Problem Solving Real World

8. Tickets to a movie cost $8 each. Write an equation for the function that gives the total cost y in dollars for an order of x tickets.

9. Write an equation for the function shown in the table. Then use the equation to find the number of bananas that can be bought for $9.

Cost of bananas (dollars), x	1	2	3	4
Number of bananas, y	3	6	9	12

Lesson Check

1. Which equation represents the function shown in the table?

x	5	6	7	8
y	15	18	21	24

   (A) $y = 2x$

   (B) $y = 3x$

   (C) $y = x + 10$

   (D) $y = 2x + 5$

2. There is a one-time fee of $20 to rent a moving truck. The cost of using the truck is $3 per mile. What is the equation for the function that gives the total cost y in dollars for renting a moving truck and driving it x miles?

   (A) $y = 20x + 3$

   (B) $y = 20x - 3$

   (C) $y = 3x + 20$

   (D) $y = 3x \times 20$

Spiral Review

3. Which of the following is a prime number?

   (A) 31

   (B) 27

   (C) 25

   (D) 21

4. Which of the following shows the Commutative Property?

   (A) $3 + 6 = 6 - 3$

   (B) $3 \times 6 = 6 \div 3$

   (C) $3 \times 6 = 6 - 3 \times (3 \times 2)$

   (D) $3 \times 6 = 6 \times 3$

5. Eva begins an 8 week training program to improve her health. By the end of the first week, she can do 10 sit-ups in a row. By the end of the second week, she can do 15 sit-ups in a row. By the end of the third week, she can do 20 sit-ups in a row. If Eva continues at this rate, how many sit-ups can she do in a row by the end of the training program?

6. Eric makes a pyramid out of playing cards. There are 2 cards in the first layer, 4 cards in the second layer, and 6 cards in the third layer. Write a rule for the pattern. Then give the number of cards that are in the tenth layer.

Name _____

Relate Fractions and Whole Numbers

Essential Question When might you use a fraction greater than 1 or a whole number?

Learning Objective You will locate and draw points as fractions and whole numbers on a number line and then use models to write fractions greater than 1.

⚷ Unlock the Problem

Elliott ran 1 mile and Amy ran $\frac{8}{8}$ of a mile. Do Elliott and Amy run the same distance?

🔑 **Locate 1 and $\frac{8}{8}$ on a number line.**

- Shade 8 lengths of $\frac{1}{8}$ and label the number line.

- Draw a point at 1 and $\frac{8}{8}$.

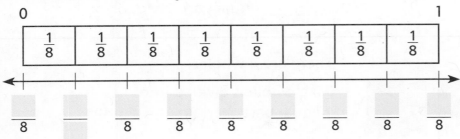

Math Idea
If two numbers are located at the same point on a number line, then they are equal and represent the same distance.

Since the distance _____ and _____ end at the same point, they are equal.

So, Elliott and Amy ran the _____ distance.

Try This! Complete the number line. Locate and draw points at $\frac{3}{6}$, $\frac{6}{6}$, and 1.

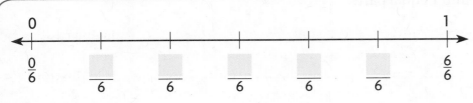

Ⓐ Are $\frac{3}{6}$ and 1 equal? Explain.

Think: Do the numbers end at the same point?

_____

_____

So, $\frac{3}{6}$ and 1 are _____.

Ⓑ Are $\frac{6}{6}$ and 1 equal? Explain.

Think: Do the numbers end at the same point?

_____

_____

So, $\frac{6}{6}$ and 1 are _____.

CONNECT The number of equal parts the whole is divided into is the denominator of a fraction. The number of parts being counted is the numerator. A **fraction greater than 1** has a numerator greater than its denominator.

🔒 Examples

Each shape is 1 whole. Write a whole number and a fraction greater than 1 for the parts that are shaded.

A

There are 3 wholes.

Each whole is divided into 4 equal parts, or fourths.

$3 = \frac{12}{4}$

There are _____ equal parts shaded.

B

There are 4 wholes.

Each whole is divided into 1 equal part.

$4 = \frac{4}{1}$

There are _____ equal parts shaded.

1. Explain what *each whole is divided into 1 equal part* means in Example B.

_____

_____

Read Math

Read $\frac{3}{1}$ as *three ones*.

2. How do you divide a whole into 1 equal part?

_____

_____

Try This!

Each shape is 1 whole. Write a whole number and a fraction greater than 1 for the parts that are shaded.

$\boxed{} = \dfrac{}{}$

Name _____

1. Each shape is 1 whole. Write a whole number and a fraction greater than 1 for the parts that are shaded.

There are _____ wholes.

Each whole is divided into _____ equal parts.

There are _____ equal parts shaded.

□ = □/□

Use the number line to find whether the two numbers are equal. Write *equal* or *not equal*.

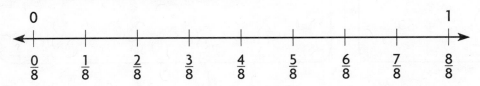

0   1

$\frac{0}{8}$ $\frac{1}{8}$ $\frac{2}{8}$ $\frac{3}{8}$ $\frac{4}{8}$ $\frac{5}{8}$ $\frac{6}{8}$ $\frac{7}{8}$ $\frac{8}{8}$

2. 1 and $\frac{8}{8}$ _____   ✓ 3. $\frac{1}{8}$ and 1 _____   ✓ 4. $\frac{4}{8}$ and $\frac{8}{8}$ _____

On Your Own

Use the number line to find whether the two numbers are equal. Write *equal* or *not equal*.

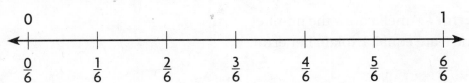

0   1

$\frac{0}{6}$ $\frac{1}{6}$ $\frac{2}{6}$ $\frac{3}{6}$ $\frac{4}{6}$ $\frac{5}{6}$ $\frac{6}{6}$

Math Talk   Process Standards ①

Evaluate How do you know whether the two fractions are equal or not equal when using a number line?

5. 1 and $\frac{5}{6}$ _____   6. $\frac{6}{6}$ and 1 _____   7. $\frac{0}{6}$ and 1 _____

Each shape is 1 whole. Write a fraction or a fraction greater than 1 for the parts that are shaded.

8.   3 = _____

9.   2 = _____

10.   3 = _____

11.   1 = _____

PROCESS STANDARDS 6 Make Connections Draw a model of the fraction or fraction greater than 1. Then write it as a whole number.

12. $\frac{10}{5}$ = _____

13. $\frac{3}{1}$ = _____

14. $\frac{15}{3}$ = _____

15. $\frac{4}{4}$ = _____

Problem Solving • Applications

16. **GO DEEPER** Kumar rode his bike around a bike trail that was $\frac{1}{5}$ of a mile long. He rode around the trail 15 times. Write a fraction greater than 1 for the distance. How many miles did Kumar ride?

_____

17. **THINK SMARTER** **What's the Error?** Amelia drew the number line below. She said that $\frac{1}{8}$ and 0 are equal. Explain her error.

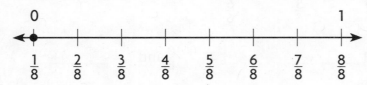

_____

18. **THINK SMARTER** Each shape is 1 whole. Which numbers name the parts that are shaded? Mark all that apply.

(A) 4   (C) $\frac{26}{6}$ (E) $\frac{6}{4}$

(B) 6   (D) $\frac{24}{6}$

Name _____

Relate Fractions and Whole Numbers

Use the number line to find whether the two numbers are equal. Write *equal* or *not equal*.

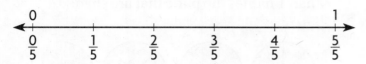

Learning Objective You will locate and draw points as fractions and whole numbers on a number line and then use models to write fractions greater than 1.

1. $\frac{0}{5}$ and 1

2. 1 and $\frac{5}{5}$

3. $\frac{1}{5}$ and $\frac{5}{5}$

_____ not equal _____

_____

_____

Each shape is 1 whole. Write a fraction or a fraction greater than 1 for the parts that are shaded.

4.

$1 =$ _____

5.

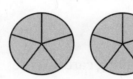
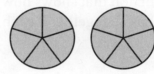

$4 =$ _____

 Problem Solving *Real World*

6. Kim jogged along a trail that was $\frac{1}{8}$ of a mile long. She jogged along the trail 16 times. How many miles did Kim jog?

_____

7. Will ran around a track that was $\frac{1}{4}$ of a mile long. He ran around the track 12 times. How many miles did Will run?

_____

8. **WRITE** ▸*Math* Write a problem that uses a fraction greater than 1.

_____

_____

Lesson Check

1. Each shape is 1 whole. What fraction greater than 1 names the parts that are shaded?

_____

2. Each shape is 1 whole. What fraction greater than 1 names the parts that are shaded?

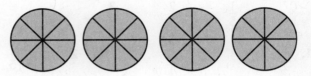

_____

Spiral Review

3. Miley has d decks of playing cards. Write an equation for a function that shows how many c cards Miley has all together if each deck has 52 cards.

_____

_____

4. In the NBA, each team is allowed to have 12 active players. There are 30 teams in the NBA. What is the maximum number of active players that can be in the NBA?

_____

_____

5. The average temperature on the planet Mercury is 167°C. The average temperature on the planet Venus is 462°C. On average, how much hotter is Venus than Mercury?

_____

6. There are 4 students in each small reading group. There are 24 students in all. How many reading groups are there?

_____

Name _____

Fractions Greater Than 1

Essential Question When might you use a fraction greater than 1 or a mixed number?

♦ Unlock the Problem

Sarah volunteers at an animal shelter. She feeds each kitten $\frac{1}{3}$ can of food. How many cans of food does she feed 5 kittens?

- How much food does Sarah give to each kitten? _____
- How many kittens does she feed?

_____

🔑 One Way Make a model.

- Shade $\frac{1}{3}$ for the amount of food Sarah gives to each of the 5 kittens.

- Then count the number of shaded pieces.

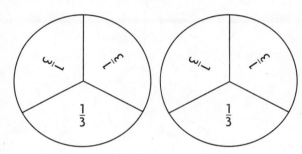

Think: $\frac{3}{3} = 1$

One whole and two thirds are shaded.

Write: $1\frac{2}{3}$

_____ pieces are shaded.

So, _____ is shaded. $\frac{5}{3} =$ _____

The number $\frac{5}{3}$ is a fraction greater than 1. A fraction greater than 1 has a numerator that is greater than its denominator.

The number $1\frac{2}{3}$ is a mixed number. A **mixed number** has a whole number and a fraction.

So, Sarah gives 5 kittens _____, or _____, cans of food.

Read Math

Read $1\frac{2}{3}$ as *one and two thirds.*

🔓 Another Way   Use a number line.

Sarah walked to raise money for the animal shelter. She earned a prize for every $\frac{1}{3}$ mile she walked. If she earned 5 prizes, how many miles did Sarah walk?

- Draw a jump of $\frac{1}{3}$ on the number line.

- Continue to draw jumps until there is a jump for each prize Sarah earned.

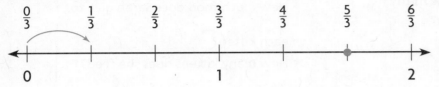

There are _____ jumps of $\frac{1}{3}$ on the number line.

There are _____ jumps past 1 on the number line.

You can say the jumps end at $\frac{5}{3}$ or $1\frac{2}{3}$ on the number line.

So, Sarah walked _____, or _____, miles.

Share and Show 🖊 MATH BOARD

1. Each circle is 1 whole. Write a mixed number for the parts that are shaded. _____

   Think: There are $\frac{7}{4}$ in all.

 Math Talk Explain how you know whether a fraction can be renamed as a mixed number.

Each shape is 1 whole. Write a mixed number and a fraction greater than 1 for the parts that are shaded.

2. _____

🔵 3. _____

4. _____

🔵 5.  _____

Name _____

On Your Own

Each shape is 1 whole. Write a mixed number and a
fraction greater than 1 for the parts that are shaded.

6. 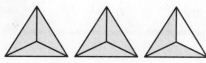 _____

7. 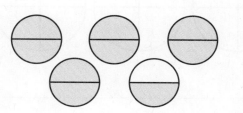 _____

_____

8. 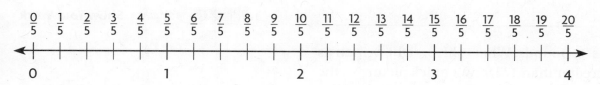 _____

_____

9. 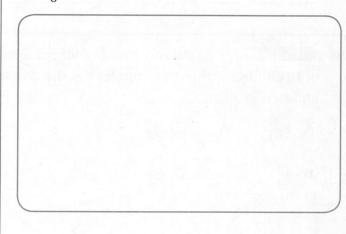 _____

_____

Use the number line for 10–13.
Write the fraction greater than 1 as a mixed number.

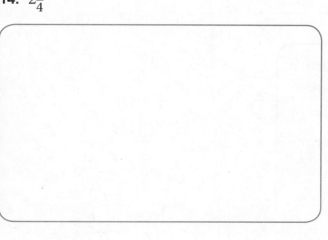

$$\frac{0}{5} \quad \frac{1}{5} \quad \frac{2}{5} \quad \frac{3}{5} \quad \frac{4}{5} \quad \frac{5}{5} \quad \frac{6}{5} \quad \frac{7}{5} \quad \frac{8}{5} \quad \frac{9}{5} \quad \frac{10}{5} \quad \frac{11}{5} \quad \frac{12}{5} \quad \frac{13}{5} \quad \frac{14}{5} \quad \frac{15}{5} \quad \frac{16}{5} \quad \frac{17}{5} \quad \frac{18}{5} \quad \frac{19}{5} \quad \frac{20}{5}$$

0   1   2   3   4

10. $\frac{6}{5}$ _____

11. $\frac{13}{5}$ _____

12. $\frac{9}{5}$ _____

13. $\frac{17}{5}$ _____

GO DEEPER Draw a quick picture to show the mixed number. Then write
the mixed number as a fraction greater than 1.

14. $2\frac{2}{4}$

_____

15. $1\frac{5}{6}$

_____

Problem Solving • Applications

Use the table for 16–17.

Weights of Kittens	
Name	**Weight (in pounds)**
Timber	$\frac{11}{4}$
Kally	$\frac{9}{6}$
Tabby	$\frac{10}{3}$

16. The table shows the weights of some kittens. Shade the model to show Timber's weight. Then write the weight as a mixed number.

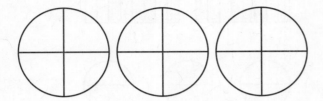

_____

17. **GO DEEPER** Which kitten weighs between 1 and 2 pounds?

_____

18. Max weighs $3\frac{1}{2}$ pounds. What is his weight written as a fraction greater than 1? Draw a quick picture in the workspace to solve.

_____

19. **WRITE** ▸ _Math_ Buttercup is a cat at the animal shelter. She weighs $2\frac{5}{8}$ pounds. Is her weight closer to 2 pounds or 3 pounds?

_____

_____

20. **THINK SMARTER** Ms. Adams gave $\frac{1}{4}$ of an apple to each of 10 children. How many apples did she give to the children in all?

  Ⓐ $1\frac{4}{10}$ Ⓒ $2\frac{1}{4}$

  Ⓑ $1\frac{2}{4}$ Ⓓ $2\frac{2}{4}$

WRITE ▸ _Math_ • **Show Your Work**

Fractions Greater Than 1

Learning Objective You will use objects and pictures to name and write mixed numbers and fractions greater than 1.

Each shape is 1 whole. Write a mixed number and a fraction greater than 1 for the parts that are shaded.

1.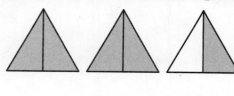

$\dfrac{5}{2}$ _____ $2\dfrac{1}{5}$ _____

2.

_____   _____

3.

_____   _____

4.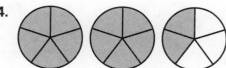

_____   _____

Use the number line for 5–7.
Write the fraction greater than 1 as a mixed number.

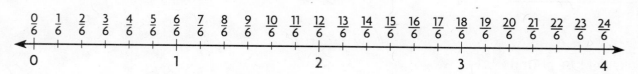

5. $\dfrac{7}{6}$

6. $\dfrac{14}{6}$

7. $\dfrac{19}{6}$

_____   _____   _____

Problem Solving

8. Rachel gave $\dfrac{1}{4}$ of a pie to each of 5 friends. How many pies did she give to her friends in all? Write the number of pies she gave as a mixed number.

_____

9. Ms. Fuller has $2\dfrac{2}{3}$ pies left over from her party. Write the number of pies left over as a fraction greater than 1.

_____

Lesson Check

1. Each shape is 1 whole. What mixed number is modeled by the shaded parts?

Ⓐ $1\frac{1}{3}$

Ⓑ $2\frac{1}{3}$

Ⓒ $2\frac{1}{2}$

Ⓓ $2\frac{2}{3}$

2. Alex's family ate $1\frac{7}{8}$ pizzas for dinner. Which shows this mixed number written as a fraction greater than 1?

Ⓐ $\frac{9}{8}$

Ⓑ $\frac{15}{8}$

Ⓒ $\frac{16}{8}$

Ⓓ $\frac{17}{8}$

Spiral Review

3. Add.

$$175{,}842$$
$$+\ 254{,}119$$

4. Dylan has read 18 books. Kylie has read twice as many books as Dylan. How many books has Kylie read?

5. Tyler challenges himself to read 35 pages per day. Which of the following is the equation for the function for the pages p that Tyler will read in d days?

Ⓐ $d = 35p$

Ⓑ $p = 35d$

Ⓒ $p = 35 + d$

Ⓓ $d = 35 \div p$

6. Matt bought a yo-yo for $2.59. How much change did he get from $3.00?

Ⓐ $1.51

Ⓑ $1.41

Ⓒ $0.51

Ⓓ $0.41

Name _____

Compare Fractions Using 0, $\frac{1}{2}$, and 1 as Benchmarks

Essential Question How can you use models and benchmarks to compare fractions?

Learning Objective You will compare two fractions by using fraction circles, number lines and 0, 1 and $\frac{1}{2}$ as benchmarks.

Benchmarks are numbers that are easy to work with. The numbers 0, $\frac{1}{2}$, and 1 are benchmarks that make it easier for you to compare fractions.

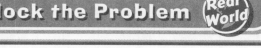

Olivia ordered a pizza. She ate $\frac{5}{8}$ of it. Did Olivia eat more than or less than $\frac{1}{2}$ of her pizza?

🔑 **Use benchmarks and fraction circles.**

Ⓐ **Compare $\frac{5}{8}$ and $\frac{1}{2}$.**

Olivia ate _____ of her pizza.

Is $\frac{5}{8}$ greater than or less than $\frac{1}{2}$?

_____

So, Olivia ate _____ $\frac{1}{2}$ of her pizza.

Lexi ate $\frac{7}{8}$ of her pizza. Did Lexi eat more than or less than 1 whole pizza?

Ⓑ **Compare $\frac{7}{8}$ and 1.**

Lexi ate _____ of her pizza.

Is $\frac{7}{8}$ greater than or less than 1?

_____

So, Lexi ate _____ 1 whole pizza.

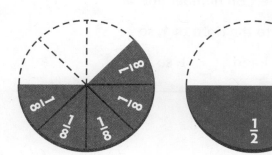

Ethan ate $\frac{1}{8}$ of his pizza. Did Ethan eat almost none of his pizza?

Ⓒ **Compare $\frac{1}{8}$ and 0.**

Ethan ate _____ of his pizza.

Is $\frac{1}{8}$ a little more than 0? _____

So, Ethan ate _____ of his pizza.

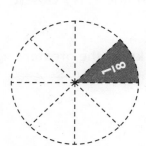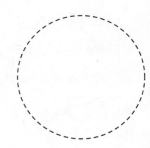

© Houghton Mifflin Harcourt Publishing Company

Use benchmarks and number lines.

Ⓐ Compare $\frac{4}{5}$ and $\frac{5}{3}$.

• Circle $\frac{4}{5}$ on number line **L**.

$\frac{4}{5}$ is to the left of 1, so $\frac{4}{5}$ ◯ 1.

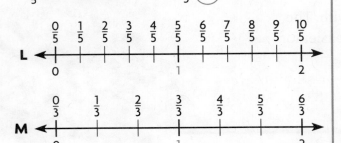

• Circle $\frac{5}{3}$ on number line **M**.

$\frac{5}{3}$ is to the right of 1, so $\frac{5}{3}$ ◯ 1.

$\frac{4}{5}$ ◯ 1 and $\frac{5}{3}$ ◯ 1, so $\frac{4}{5}$ ◯ $\frac{5}{3}$.

Ⓑ Compare $\frac{2}{6}$ and $\frac{3}{4}$.

• Circle $\frac{2}{6}$ on number line **S**.

$\frac{2}{6}$ is to the left of $\frac{1}{2}$, so $\frac{2}{6}$ ◯ $\frac{1}{2}$.

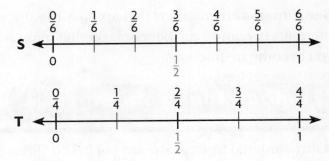

• Circle $\frac{3}{4}$ on number line **T**.

$\frac{3}{4}$ is to the right of $\frac{1}{2}$, so $\frac{3}{4}$ ◯ $\frac{1}{2}$.

$\frac{2}{6}$ ◯ $\frac{1}{2}$ and $\frac{3}{4}$ ◯ $\frac{1}{2}$, so $\frac{2}{6}$ ◯ $\frac{3}{4}$.

Ⓒ Compare $\frac{1}{10}$ and $\frac{3}{5}$.

• Circle $\frac{1}{10}$ on the number line **X**.

Is $\frac{1}{10}$ closest to 0 , $\frac{1}{2}$, or 1? _____

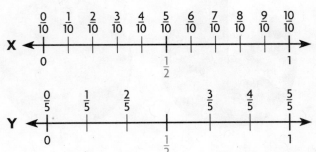

• Circle $\frac{3}{5}$ on the number line **Y**. Is $\frac{3}{5}$ closest

to 0, $\frac{1}{2}$ or 1? _____

Since $0 < \frac{1}{2}$, now you know the greater

fraction is closest to $\frac{1}{2}$.

So, $\frac{1}{10}$ ◯ $\frac{3}{5}$.

Use reasoning.

Ⓓ Compare $\frac{3}{8}$ and $\frac{5}{6}$.

• First, look at $\frac{3}{8}$. **Think:** $\frac{1}{2}$ of 8 = 4

So, $\frac{4}{8}$ is the same as $\frac{1}{2}$. Now you know

$\frac{3}{8}$ ◯ $\frac{1}{2}$.

• Then look at $\frac{5}{6}$. **Think:** $\frac{1}{2}$ of 6 = 3

So, $\frac{3}{6}$ is the same as $\frac{1}{2}$. Now you know

$\frac{5}{6}$ ◯ $\frac{1}{2}$.

So, $\frac{3}{8}$ ◯ $\frac{5}{6}$.

• If the numerator *is less than* half the denominator, the fraction is less than $\frac{1}{2}$.

• If the numerator *is greater than* half the denominator, the fraction is greater than $\frac{1}{2}$.

Math Talk **Explain** how you know that a fraction is less than $\frac{1}{2}$ when the numerator is less than half the denominator.

Name _____

1. Use the models to compare $\frac{7}{8}$ and $\frac{1}{2}$.

$\frac{7}{8}$ ◯ $\frac{1}{2}$

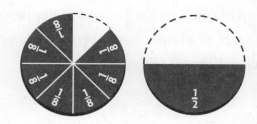

Use the benchmarks on the number line to help you compare. Write < or >.

```
 ◄──┼────────┼────────┼────────┼────────┼──►
    0        1/2       1       1 1/2      2
```

✓2. $\frac{1}{3}$ ◯ $\frac{3}{6}$ 3. $\frac{3}{10}$ ◯ $\frac{3}{2}$ ✓4. $\frac{2}{8}$ ◯ $\frac{0}{5}$ 5. $\frac{2}{6}$ ◯ $\frac{2}{4}$

> **Math Talk** Name one fraction greater than $\frac{1}{2}$ and one fraction less than $\frac{1}{2}$. **Explain** your choices.

On Your Own

Compare. Write < or >.

6. $\frac{7}{8}$ ◯ $\frac{2}{4}$ 7. $\frac{0}{1}$ ◯ $\frac{1}{2}$ 8. $\frac{9}{10}$ ◯ $\frac{2}{5}$ 9. $\frac{1}{6}$ ◯ $\frac{2}{3}$

10. $\frac{3}{8}$ ◯ $\frac{11}{10}$ 11. $\frac{3}{4}$ ◯ $\frac{2}{6}$ 12. $\frac{3}{6}$ ◯ $\frac{2}{5}$ 13. $\frac{6}{8}$ ◯ $\frac{8}{6}$

14. **GO DEEPER** Ms. Hopper wrote the following fractions on the board.

$\frac{2}{25}$, $\frac{51}{100}$, $\frac{18}{25}$, $\frac{35}{100}$, $\frac{12}{10}$, $\frac{5}{3}$, $\frac{3}{8}$, $\frac{1}{100}$, $\frac{3}{10}$, $\frac{99}{100}$

Sort the fractions into four groups: close to 0, less than $\frac{1}{2}$, greater than $\frac{1}{2}$, and greater than 1. Complete the chart. Some fractions may be used more than once.

Close to 0	
Less Than $\frac{1}{2}$	
Greater Than $\frac{1}{2}$	
Greater Than 1	

Problem Solving • Applications

15. A group of students ate $\frac{5}{8}$ of a large pepperoni pizza and $\frac{1}{4}$ of a large cheese pizza. Which pizza had a smaller part left?

_____

16. Mason runs $\frac{4}{10}$ mile. Madison runs $\frac{3}{4}$ mile.

Who runs farther? _____

17. **GO DEEPER** **Pose a Problem** Look back at Problem 16. Write a similar problem by changing the fractions of the mile they run, so the solution is different from Problem 16.

_____

_____

18. Ms. Endo made two pies the same size. Her family ate $\frac{1}{3}$ of the apple pie and $\frac{3}{4}$ of the cherry pie. Which pie had more left over?

_____

19. **WRITE** ▸*Math* **What's the Error?**
Tom has two pieces of wood to build a birdhouse. One piece is $\frac{3}{4}$ yard long. The other piece is $\frac{4}{8}$ yard long. Tom says both pieces of wood are the same length. **Explain** his error.

_____

_____

20. **THINK SMARTER** Michael and Ava are playing a game with fraction pieces. Which statement is NOT correct?

Ⓐ $\frac{5}{6} < \frac{1}{2}$ Ⓒ $\frac{5}{6} > 0$

Ⓑ $\frac{3}{6} = \frac{1}{2}$ Ⓓ $\frac{5}{6} < 1$

Name _____

Compare Fractions Using 0, $\frac{1}{2}$, and 1 as Benchmarks

Learning Objective You will compare two fractions by using fraction circles, number lines and 0, 1, and $\frac{1}{2}$ as benchmarks.

Use the benchmarks on the number line to help you compare. Write < or >.

1. Compare $\frac{2}{8}$ and $\frac{3}{4}$.

$\frac{2}{8}$ $\boxed{<}$ $\frac{3}{4}$

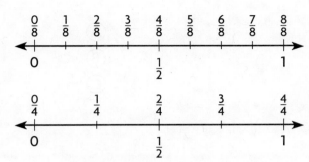

Compare. Write < or >.

2. $\frac{1}{8}$ $\boxed{<}$ $\frac{6}{10}$

3. $\frac{4}{6}$ $\boxed{>}$ $\frac{1}{3}$

4. $\frac{2}{8}$ $\boxed{<}$ $\frac{1}{2}$

5. $\frac{3}{5}$ $\boxed{<}$ $\frac{3}{3}$

6. $\frac{4}{3}$ $\boxed{>}$ $\frac{5}{10}$

7. $\frac{5}{1}$ $\boxed{>}$ $\frac{1}{5}$

8. $\frac{4}{6}$ $\boxed{<}$ $\frac{7}{5}$

9. $\frac{0}{6}$ $\boxed{<}$ $\frac{3}{8}$

10. $\frac{11}{10}$ $\boxed{>}$ $\frac{1}{4}$

Problem Solving · Real World

11. Erika ran $\frac{3}{8}$ mile. Maria ran $\frac{3}{4}$ mile. Which is the greater distance?

$\frac{3}{4}$ is the greater distance.

12. Carlos finished $\frac{1}{3}$ of his art project on Monday. Tyler finished $\frac{1}{2}$ of his art project on Monday. Who finished more of his art project on Monday?

Tyler finished more of his art project on Monday, because $\frac{1}{2}$ is more than $\frac{1}{3}$.

Lesson Check

1. Which symbol makes the statement true?

   $\frac{4}{6}$ ● $\frac{3}{8}$

   (A) >

   (B) <

   (C) =

2. Which symbol makes the statement true?

   $\frac{3}{5}$ ● $\frac{3}{2}$

   (A) >

   (B) <

   (C) =

Spiral Review

3. Which is not a factor of 42?

   (A) 3

   (B) 14

   (C) 21

   (D) 31

4. Find the quotient.

   $942 \div 6 =$ ■

   (A) 207

   (B) 157

   (C) 150

   (D) 17

5. Daniel competes in the high jump for his school's track team. He jumps $1\frac{3}{10}$ meters on his first attempt. He jumps $1\frac{7}{10}$ meters on his second attempt. How many meters more does Daniel jump on his second attempt?

   _____

6. Pilar arranges 40 tiles in an array. She places 5 tiles in each row. How many rows of 5 does Pilar make?

   _____

Name _____

Explore Decimal Place Value

Essential Question How can you find the value of a digit using its place-value position?

Learning Objective You will use words, models, standard form, and expanded form to represent decimal numbers to hundredths.

CONNECT Decimals, like whole numbers, can be written in standard form, word form, and expanded form.

 Unlock the Problem

How can you write the value of each digit in 5.76 using decimal expander strips?

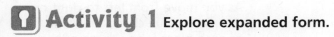 **Activity 1** Explore expanded form.

Materials ▪ decimal expander strips

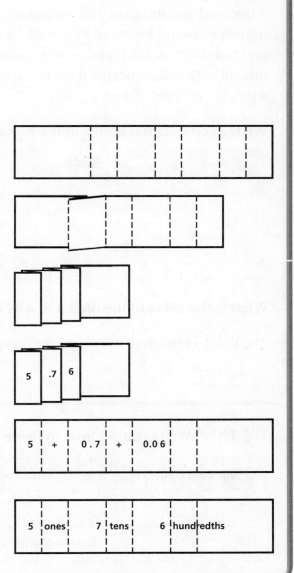

STEP 1 Place the decimal expander strip in front of you, with the largest rectangle on the left-hand side.

STEP 2 Fold along the first two dashed lines as shown, keeping the largest rectangle toward the back.

STEP 3 Continue folding along the dashed lines. Then turn the paper around so that the largest rectangle is on the right-hand side.

STEP 4 Write 5, 7, 6, placing one digit in each section, as shown. Insert a decimal point before the 7.

STEP 5 Unfold the decimal expander, and use numbers and symbols to write 5 + 0.7 + 0.06.

STEP 6 Use the second strip of paper to make another decimal expander for 5.76. This time, write the word that names the value of each digit. The strip should read 5 ones 7 tenths 6 hundredths.

- What are some other ways you can expand the decimal 5.76 by using both decimal expanders?

_____

_____

Math Talk Explain how you can write 3.5 as 35 tenths.

Example Use a place-value chart.

Shortfin mako shark teeth range in length from 0.64 centimeter to 5.08 centimeters. Eli found a shark tooth measuring 2.54 centimeters on the beach in Venice, Florida, the shark tooth capital of the world.

You can use a place-value chart to help you understand decimal place value.

A decimal amount uses place value to represent values less than one, such as tenths and hundredths. Each place-value position is related to the place beside it based on a ten-to-one rule.

▲ A shortfin mako shark may grow 20,000 teeth during its lifetime!

Ten-to-One Rule

As you move from left to right on the place-value chart, the value of each place is one tenth of the value of the place to its left.

Write each decimal above in the place-value chart.

Ones	.	Tenths	Hundredths

 ERROR Alert

Always place the decimal point between the ones digit and the tenths digit.

decimal point
↓
0.1
↑

A zero is used to show there are no ones.

What is the value of the digit 4 in 2.54?

The value of the digit 4 is _____ hundredths,

or _____ .

Try This! Write the decimal in three forms.

Standard Form	Expanded Form	Word Form
0.6		six tenths
	9 + 0.4	nine and four tenths
0.28	0.2 + 0.08	
3.75		three and seventy-five hundredths

Name _____

1. What is the place-value position

   of the digit 8 in 0.98? _____

Ones	.	Tenths	Hundredths
0	.	9	8

Write the value of the underlined digit.

2. 2.<u>1</u>   3. 0.0<u>9</u>   4. 6.5<u>4</u>   ⊘ 5. 0.<u>3</u>

_____   _____   _____   _____

Write the number in two other forms.

6. 3.0 + 0.9 + 0.02   ⊘ 7. seventeen hundredths

_____   _____

_____   _____

Math Talk In the whole number 277, the value of each digit is 10 times greater than the place-value position to its right. **Explain** why, in the decimal 2.77, the value of the digit 7 in the tenths place is 10 times greater than the value of the digit 7 in the hundredths place.

On Your Own

Write the value of the underlined digit.

8. 8.7<u>1</u>   9. 10.<u>4</u>   10. 0.6<u>3</u>   11. 0.<u>5</u>

_____   _____   _____   _____

Write the number in standard form.

12. 8 ones 1 tenth 2 hundredths _____   13. 90 + 2 + 0.67 _____

14. 3.2 + 0.01 _____   15. 83 hundredths _____

Practice: Copy and Solve **Write the number in two other forms.**

16. 8.26   17. one and two tenths

18. 10 + 6 + 0.7 + 0.02   19. 95.31

GO DEEPER **Algebra** **Write the unknown decimal.**

20. $7.16 = 7 +$ _____ $+ 0.06$

21. $0.58 = 0.5 +$ _____

22. _____ $= 4 + 0.02$

23. $0.63 =$ _____ $+ 0.03$

24. _____ $= 10 + 0.9$

25. $12.07 = 12 +$ _____

Problem Solving · Real World

Use the chart for 26–28.

26. A marine researcher recorded the lengths of some sharks he observed offshore. The length of which shark has the digit 7 in the tenths place?

_____

27. What is the length of the blackfin shark written in expanded form?

_____

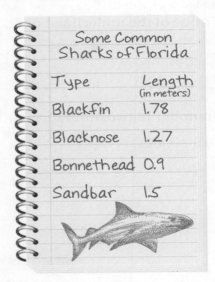

Some Common Sharks of Florida

Type	Length (in meters)
Blackfin	1.78
Blacknose	1.27
Bonnethead	0.9
Sandbar	1.5

28. **GO DEEPER** **What's the Error?** Randy said that the blacknose shark is one and twenty-seven tenths meters in length. Describe Randy's error.

_____

_____

_____

_____

WRITE ⟩ *Math* • **Show Your Work**

29. **GO DEEPER** **What's the Question?** The answer is one and six hundredths.

_____

_____

30. **THINK SMARTER** The average annual precipitation in Miami, Florida, is 55.91 inches. What is the value of the digit 9 in the decimal 55.91?

(**A**) nine tens

(**C**) nine tenths

(**B**) nine ones

(**D**) nine hundredths

Explore Decimal Place Value

Learning Objective You will use words, models, standard form, and expanded form to represent decimal numbers to hundredths.

Write the value of the underlined digit.

1. 6.2<u>4</u>

4 hundredths, or 0.04

2. 3.<u>2</u>

_____

3. 9.0<u>7</u>

_____

4. 0.4<u>8</u>

_____

5. 1.<u>6</u>5

_____

_____

6. 0.<u>9</u>

_____

_____

7. 5.1<u>3</u>

_____

_____

8. 10.<u>8</u>2

_____

_____

Write the decimal in two other forms.

9. 7.32

_____

_____

10. two and six tenths

_____

_____

11. 20 + 5 + 0.8 + 0.01

_____

_____

12. 86.04

_____

_____

Use the table below for 13 and 14.

Foot Race Times

Runner	Time (in seconds)
Erika	15.46
Andre	14.89
Conner	15.08

13. Which runner finished the race with a time that has the digit 8 in the hundredths place?

_____

14. What is Erika's time written in expanded form?

_____

Lesson Check

1. The Daytona International Speedway has a road course that is 3.56 miles in length. What is the value of the digit 6 in 3.56?

Ⓐ six tens

Ⓑ six ones

Ⓒ six tenths

Ⓓ six hundredths

2. At the 2008 Olympics in Beijing, the U.S. men's 400-meter relay team finished in first place by eight hundredths of a second. What is eight hundredths written in standard form?

Ⓐ 0.008

Ⓑ 0.08

Ⓒ 0.8

Ⓓ 800

Spiral Review

3. Which of the following numbers has the digit 9 in the ten thousands place?

Ⓐ 39,042

Ⓑ 40,923

Ⓒ 54,093

Ⓓ 93,420

4. Which of the following fractions are equivalent?

Ⓐ $\frac{4}{10}, \frac{2}{5}$

Ⓑ $\frac{5}{6}, \frac{25}{40}$

Ⓒ $\frac{1}{4}, \frac{12}{50}$

Ⓓ $\frac{20}{100}, \frac{2}{5}$

5. The total land area of Florida is 54,136 square miles. What is the value of the digit 4 in the number 54,136?

6. Write the fraction that is equivalent to the shaded area of the rectangle below.

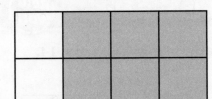

Name _____

Draw Quadrilaterals

Essential Question How can you draw quadrilaterals?

🔑 Unlock the Problem

CONNECT You have learned to classify quadrilaterals by the number of pairs of opposite sides that are parallel, by the number of pairs of sides of equal length, and by the number of right angles.

How can you draw quadrilaterals?

🔒 Activity 1 Use grid paper to draw quadrilaterals.

Materials ■ ruler

- Use a ruler to draw line segments from points *A* to *B*, from *B* to *C*, from *C* to *D*, and from *D* to *A*.

- Write the name of your quadrilateral.

_____

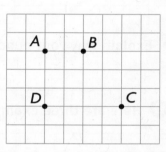

🔒 Activity 2 Draw a shape that does not belong.

Materials ■ ruler

A Here are three examples of a parallelogram. Draw an example of a quadrilateral that is not a parallelogram.

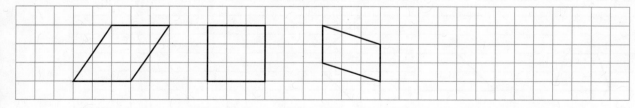

- Explain why your quadrilateral is not a parallelogram.

_____

_____

B Here are three examples of a square. Draw a quadrilateral that is not a square.

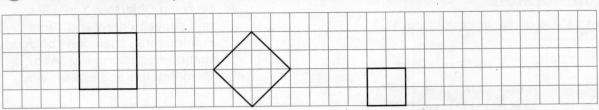

- Explain why your quadrilateral is not a square.

_____

C Here are three examples of a rectangle. Draw a quadrilateral that is not a rectangle.

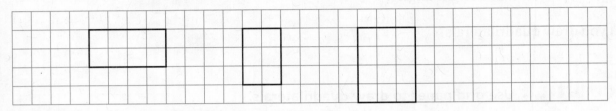

- Explain why your quadrilateral is not a rectangle.

_____

D Here are three examples of a rhombus. Draw a quadrilateral that is not a rhombus.

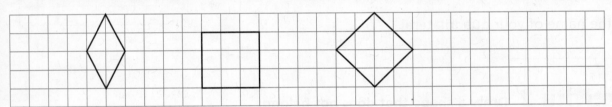

- Explain why your quadrilateral is not a rhombus.

_____

E Here are three examples of a trapezoid. Draw a quadrilateral that is not a trapezoid.

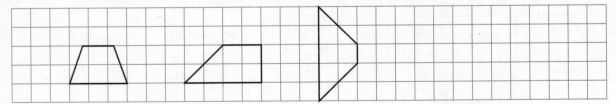

- Explain why your quadrilateral is not a trapezoid.

_____

 Math Talk

Process Standards **3**

Compare Representations Compare your drawings with your classmates. Explain how your drawings are alike and how they are different.

Name _____

1. Choose four endpoints, and connect them to make a parallelogram.

   Think: A parallelogram has 2 pairs of parallel sides and 2 pairs of sides of equal length.

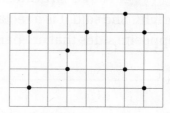

Draw a quadrilateral that is described.
Name the quadrilateral you drew.

2. 2 pairs of sides of equal length

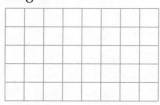

   Name _____

3. 4 sides of equal length

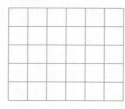

   Name _____

Math Talk

Process Standards ③

Compare Explain one way the quadrilaterals you drew are alike and one way they are different.

On Your Own

Practice: Copy and Solve Use grid paper to draw a quadrilateral that is described. Name the quadrilateral you drew.

4. exactly 1 pair of opposite sides that are parallel

5. 4 right angles

6. 2 pairs of sides of equal length

Draw a quadrilateral that does not belong. Then explain why.

7.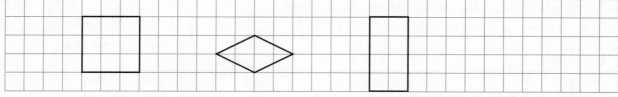

_____

8.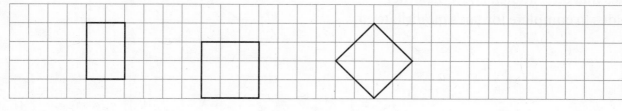

_____

Problem Solving • Applications

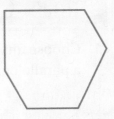

9. **PROCESS STANDARDS ③ Make Arguments** Jacki drew the shape at the right. She said it is a rectangle because it has 2 pairs of opposite sides that are parallel. Describe her error.

_____

_____

10. **GO DEEPER** Adam drew three quadrilaterals. One quadrilateral has no pairs of parallel sides, one quadrilateral has exactly 1 pair of opposite sides that are parallel, and the last quadrilateral has 2 pairs of opposite sides that are parallel. Draw the three quadrilaterals that Adam could have drawn. Name them.

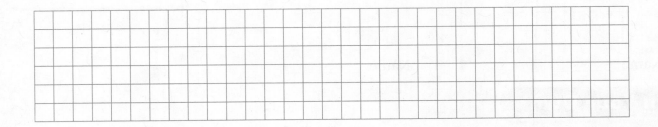

_____   _____   _____

11. **THINK SMARTER** Amy has 4 straws of equal length. Name all the quadrilaterals that can be made using these 4 straws.

_____ Amy cuts one of the straws in half. She uses the two halves and two of the other straws to make a quadrilateral. Name all the quadrilaterals that can be made using these 4 straws.

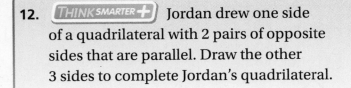

_____

12. **THINK SMARTER ＋** Jordan drew one side of a quadrilateral with 2 pairs of opposite sides that are parallel. Draw the other 3 sides to complete Jordan's quadrilateral.

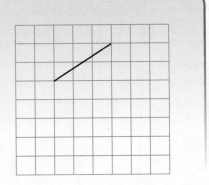

Draw Quadrilaterals

Learning Objective You will use grid paper to draw and name quadrilaterals then draw polygons that do not belong in a set of quadrilaterals and explain why.

Draw a quadrilateral that is described.
Name the quadrilateral you drew.

1. has 4 right angles and 2 pairs of sides of equal length

_____rectangle_____

2. only 1 pair of opposite sides that are parallel

_____

Draw a quadrilateral that does not belong.
Then explain why.

3.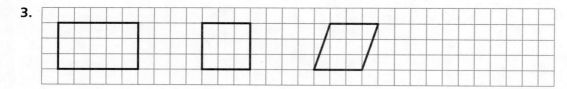

_____

_____

_____

Problem Solving Real World

4. Layla drew a quadrilateral with 4 sides of equal length and 2 pairs of parallel sides. What quadrilateral best describes her drawing?

_____

_____

5. **WRITE** *Math* Draw a quadrilateral that is NOT a rectangle. Describe your shape, and explain why it is not a rectangle.

_____

_____

Lesson Check

1. Chloe drew a quadrilateral with 2 pairs of opposite sides that are parallel. Name all the shapes that could be Chloe's quadrilateral.

    _____

    _____

2. Mike drew a quadrilateral with four right angles. Name all the shapes he could have drawn.

    _____

    _____

Spiral Review

3. What is the name of the quadrilateral that always has 4 right angles and 4 sides of equal length?

    _____

4. Mark drew two lines that form a right angle. What words describe the lines Mark drew?

    _____

5. Mary ate $\frac{1}{8}$ of a pizza. Steven ate $\frac{1}{4}$ of the same pizza. How much more pizza did Steven eat than Mary?

    (A) $\frac{1}{4}$

    (B) $\frac{1}{6}$

    (C) $\frac{3}{8}$

    (D) $\frac{1}{8}$

6. Which are factors of 24?

    (A) 1, 2, 3, 4, 6, 8, 12, 24

    (B) 1, 2, 3, 8, 12

    (C) 1, 2, 3, 8, 12, 24

    (D) 3, 4, 6, 8

Name _____

Length

Essential Question How can you measure lengths of objects to the nearest unit?

Learning Objective You will estimate and measure lengths of objects to the nearest linear unit.

Unlock the Problem (Real World)

Linear units are used to measure length, width, height, and distance. Which customary linear unit would you use to find the shortest box that a group of markers will fit into?

Activity 1 Measure to the nearest $\frac{1}{2}$ inch, $\frac{1}{4}$ inch, and $\frac{1}{8}$ inch.

Measure the length of one marker to the nearest $\frac{1}{2}$ inch, $\frac{1}{4}$ inch, and $\frac{1}{8}$ inch to decide on the shortest box.

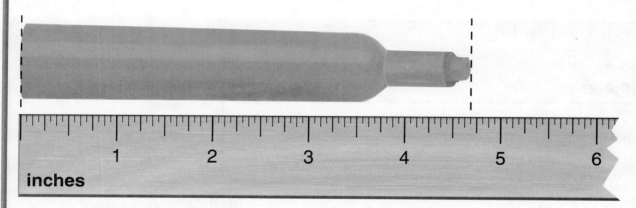

inches

Unit	What two lengths is the measurement between?	Length (to the nearest unit)	Would this box be long enough?
$\frac{1}{2}$ inch	$4\frac{1}{2}$ inches and 5 inches		
$\frac{1}{4}$ inch	_____ and _____		
$\frac{1}{8}$ inch	_____ and _____		

> **Math Talk** **Explain** how benchmarks help you select a unit of measure.

So, the shortest box that the markers will fit into must be

_____ inches tall.

- **What if** you estimated the length of the marker using a benchmark for 1 inch? What benchmark would you use? About how long is the measure?

Metric Length You can measure length, width, height, or distance using metric units. Some metric linear units are shown below. Shorter lengths, such as the yarn in Activity 1, are measured in centimeters or millimeters.

Metric Units of Length

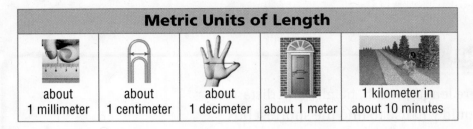

about 1 millimeter	about 1 centimeter	about 1 decimeter	about 1 meter	1 kilometer in about 10 minutes

Activity 1 Measure the yarn to the nearest centimeter and millimeter.

1 2 3 4 5 6 7 8 9 10 11 12

centimeters

Each centimeter represents 10 millimeters.

Measured to the nearest centimeter, the yarn is about _____ centimeters.

Measured to the nearest millimeter, the yarn is _____ millimeters.

Activity 2 Estimate and measure.

Math Talk Explain how you can use your estimate to determine if your measurement is reasonable.

Materials ■ 2 classroom objects ■ metric ruler ■ meterstick

Estimate and measure the width of a student desk and the length, width, or height of two other classroom objects, using the appropriate linear unit. Complete the table.

Lengths of Classroom Objects

Object	Appropriate Unit	Estimate	Actual Measure
Student desk			

- Which metric unit would you use to measure the width of

   a student desk? _____

Name _____

For 1–3, measure the length of the crayon to the nearest unit.

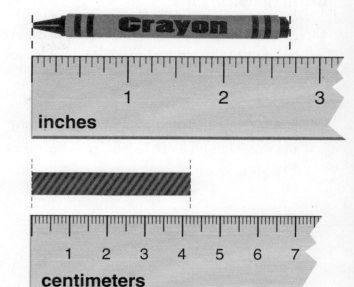

1. nearest $\frac{1}{2}$ inch _____

2. nearest $\frac{1}{4}$ inch _____

✓ 3. nearest $\frac{1}{8}$ inch _____

For 4–5, measure the length of the ribbon to the nearest unit.

4. nearest centimeter _____

✓ 5. nearest millimeter _____

On Your Own

Measure to the nearest $\frac{1}{8}$ inch and to the nearest millimeter.

6. _____

7. _____

8. _____

9. _____

10. _____

11. _____

Use an inch ruler and a metric ruler. Draw a line for each length.
Measure it to the nearest $\frac{1}{8}$ inch or millimeter with the other ruler.

12. 58 millimeters

    Customary length _____

13. $4\frac{3}{4}$ inches

    Metric length _____

Problem Solving Real World

Use the graph to solve 14–15.

14. About how many centimeters long is the ladybug? Which benchmark is this close to?

_____

15. Dalton said the monarch butterfly is about the same length as 10 ladybugs. Is he correct? **Explain.**

_____

_____

_____

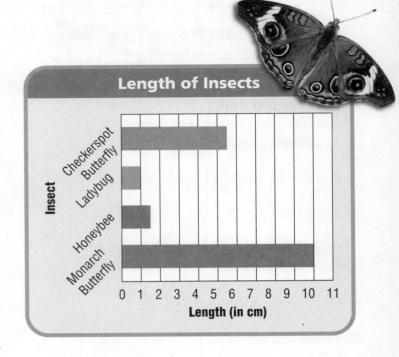

Length of Insects

Use the rulers for 16–17.

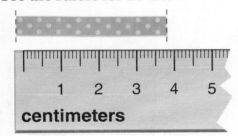

centimeters

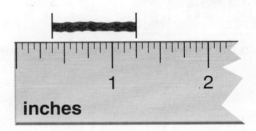

inches

16. GO DEEPER **What's the Error?** Emma measured the ribbon above. She said it was 38 millimeters long. Is Emma correct? **Explain.**

_____

_____

_____

17. GO DEEPER Tyler did not align the yarn correctly on the ruler. **Explain** how to find the length of the yarn using subtraction.

_____

_____

_____

18. THINK SMARTER What is the length of the yarn in exercise 17 to the nearest $\frac{1}{2}$ inch?

Ⓐ $\frac{1}{2}$ inch

Ⓑ 1 inch

Ⓒ $1\frac{1}{2}$ inches

Ⓓ 2 inches

Length

Learning Objective You will estimate and measure lengths of objects to the nearest linear unit.

**Estimate the length of each object in inches.
Then measure the object to the nearest unit using
a customary ruler. Complete the table.**

Item	Estimate	Nearest $\frac{1}{2}$ in.	Nearest $\frac{1}{4}$ in.	Nearest $\frac{1}{8}$ in.
1. Length of a window				
2. Height of a chair				
3. Length of a pair of scissors				
4. Width of a calculator				

**Measure the item to the nearest centimeter and to the
nearest millimeter.**

5. Length of a pencil _____

6. Width of a calculator _____

**Use an inch ruler and a metric ruler. Draw a line for each length.
Measure it to the nearest $\frac{1}{8}$ inch or millimeter with the
other ruler.**

7. $4\frac{1}{8}$ inches   Metric length _____

8. $2\frac{5}{8}$ inches   Metric length _____

9. 8 centimeters   Customary length _____

10. 49 millimeters   Customary length _____

Problem Solving Real World

11. Which unit would be most appropriate for measuring the width of a postage stamp: millimeter, centimeter, meter, or kilometer?

12. What is a good estimate for the height of a teacher's desk?

_____   _____

Lesson Check

1. Which is the best estimate for the height of a flagpole?

   Ⓐ 8 inches

   Ⓑ 8 feet

   Ⓒ 8 yards

   Ⓓ 8 miles

2. Which is the best estimate for the length of a car?

   Ⓐ 4 decimeters

   Ⓑ 4 tons

   Ⓒ 4 kilograms

   Ⓓ 4 meters

Spiral Review

3. A museum sells collector boxes for displaying rock samples. If each box holds 8 rocks, how many boxes are needed to display 456 rocks?

4. Tickets to the county fair cost $7 each. Write an equation for the function that gives the total cost, y, in dollar for an order of x tickets, plus $3 for shipping.

5. Which number is not a factor of 54?

   Ⓐ 18

   Ⓑ 13

   Ⓒ 9

   Ⓓ 2

6. Which of the following are multiples of 4?

   Ⓐ 5, 10, 15, 20

   Ⓑ 6, 10, 14, 16

   Ⓒ 8, 12, 16, 20

   Ⓓ 3, 12, 20, 28

Collect and Organize Data

Essential Question How can you collect and organize data by conducting a survey, experiments, or making an observation?

Learning Objective You will collect and organize data in tally tables and frequency tables.

Unlock the Problem (Real World)

Data is a set of numbers or pieces of information. Conducting a survey is one way to collect data. When you ask people questions and record their answers, you are conducting a survey. Making an observation is another way to collect data. When you collect data by looking at an object or event, you are making an observation. Conducting an experiment is also a way of collecting data. When conducting an experiment, the results of the experiment will be the data that is collected.

You can use a tally table and a frequency table to record the data you collect.

🔑 Activity Conduct a survey of the students in your class and record the results in a tally table and a frequency table.

STEP 1 Think of a survey question that has at least three possible answers. Write your question on the line below.

Survey question: _____

STEP 2 Complete the labels of the tally table. Include a title and headings. List at least three possible answers to your question.

_____

STEP 3 Survey the students in your class. Record the results in your tally table. Then, use your tally table to complete your frequency table.

_____

STEP 4 Analyze your data.

Which choice got the most tally marks?

_____

How many students did you survey? _____

	Tally

	Number

Math Talk Describe how your survey results compare with those of a friend.

🔓 Examples

Ⓐ Survey Questions

• **Would you rather have a brown crayon or a beautiful red crayon? (Brown Crayon, Beautiful Red Crayon)**

You **can** answer this question, but the word *beautiful* might lead you to choose the red crayon. It is not a fair question. So, this survey question **is not** a good question.

• **Do you like the color and smell of bananas? (Yes, No)**

You **cannot** answer this question if you like the color but not the smell. The question asks about too many things. So, this survey question **is not** a good question.

• **How did you get to school today? (Bus, Car, Walk, Other)**

You _____ answer this question, even if you rode a horse to school. It is fair and does not ask about too many things. So, this

survey question _____ a good question.

Ⓑ Observations

• **Record the number of phone calls you get in 1 week.**

It **is** possible to count how many calls you get each day for a week. So, this observation **is** a good way to collect data.

• **Sit in your house and record the birds that land on the roof.**

It _____ possible to see your roof from inside your house. So,

this observation _____ a good way to collect data.

Ⓒ Experiments

• **Eat a piece of broccoli to see if you like green foods.**

You **cannot** perform this experiment because there are **many** green foods, like kiwi and spinach, that do not taste like broccoli. So, this experiment **is not** a good way to collect data.

• **Toss a coin 100 times to find how many times it shows heads.**

You _____ perform this experiment because a coin has both heads and tails. The more you repeat an experiment, the better your

results are. So, this experiment _____ a good way to collect data.

Name _____

Tell if the survey question, experiment, or observation is good. Explain your reasoning.

1. What kind of pet do you like best? (Cat, Dog, Other)

_____

_____

2. Would you rather eat a boring apple or a pineapple? (Boring Apple, Pineapple)

_____

_____

3. Test many different types of soap to see which one kills the most bacteria.

_____

_____

✓ 4. Observe three turtles and record the number of seconds it takes them to each walk 2 feet.

_____

_____

Use the frequency table for 5–6.

5. Liam recorded the results of a survey of his classmates in the frequency table at the right. What survey question did Liam most likely ask?

_____

✓ 6. How many classmates were surveyed? _____

Subject	Number of Votes
Reading	4
Math	7
Science	5
Other	6

Math Talk Write an unfair survey question and **explain** why it is not fair. Then correct the question so it is fair.

On Your Own

Tell if the survey question, experiments, or observation are good. Explain your reasoning.

7. Testing many types of toothpaste to see which one whitens teeth the most.

_____

8. Do you like the feel and warmth of wool? (Yes, No)

_____

Use the tally table at the right for 9–11.

Drawing Tool	Tally
Color Pencil	JHT IIII
Crayon	JHT II
Marker	JHT II
Other	III

9. Nella recorded the results of a survey in this tally table. What survey question did she most likely ask?

_____

10. How many people were surveyed? _____

11. **GO DEEPER** **What if** Nella's survey question was, "Which two drawing tools did you use for your art project?" How many tallies would Nella record for each person she surveyed? How would that change your answer to Problem 10?

_____

12. **GO DEEPER** **WRITE** ▸ *Math* **Practice: Copy and Solve** Write a survey question about insects. Provide at least three possible answers to your question.

Problem Solving · Real World

Use the frequency table at the right for 13–17.

Vowel	Number
A	
E	
I	
O	
U	

13. Record the number of times each vowel occurs in this sentence.

14. Which vowel occurs most often? _____

15. How many vowels were there in all? _____

16. **WRITE** ▸ *Math* **Pose a Problem** Write a problem similar to Problem 15 that has 6 as its answer.

17. **THINK SMARTER +** In the frequency table above, which vowels occurred three times as much as I?

(A) A   (C) O

(B) E   (D) U

Name _____

Collect and Organize Data

Learning Objective You will collect and organize data in tally tables and frequency tables.

Tell if the survey question, experiment, or observation is good.
Explain your reasoning.

1. Where are you going for summer vacation?
   (Florida, New York, California, Staying Home)

   Not good; I cannot answer this question if I am going somewhere not listed, such as Ohio.

   _____

2. Record the number of pieces of mail you get in one week.

   _____

   _____

Use the frequency table at the right for 3 and 4.

3. Joan recorded the results of a survey of her classmates in the frequency table at the right. What survey question did Joan most likely ask?

   _____

   _____

Juice	Number
Apple	7
Orange	8
Grape	2
Other	3

4. How many classmates did Joan survey? _____

Problem Solving

Use the tally table at the right for 5–7.

5. Matt has the following stickers. Tally the number of each type of sticker Matt has.

6. Which type of sticker occurs least often? _____

7. Matt gives 3 heart stickers to a friend. How many heart stickers does he have left? _____

Sticker	Tally
☆	
⇨	
♡	
☺	
☾	

Lesson Check

1. Which of the following survey questions, experiments, or observations is good?

   (A) Do you like cheese pizza or stinky anchovy pizza better? (Cheese, Stinky Anchovy)

   (B) Record the number of steps you take each day for a month.

   (C) Observe and record the number of apples your friend eats in one week.

   (D) Observe students in your class and record how many have an older brother.

2. Carlton recorded the results of a survey of his classmates in this tally table. How many students did Carlton survey?

   (A) 10
   (B) 19
   (C) 22
   (D) 37

Movie	Tally
Comedy	JHT II
Action	JHT JHT
Drama	II
Other	III

Spiral Review

3. Which is 6 ones 4 tenths 8 hundredths written in standard form?

   (A) 4.68
   (B) 6.48
   (C) 8.64
   (D) 64.8

4. Which is an equivalent fraction to $\frac{4}{6}$?

   (A) $\frac{1}{4}$
   (B) $\frac{2}{4}$
   (C) $\frac{2}{3}$
   (D) $\frac{2}{6}$

5. At a wedding reception, there are 25 tables. Each table has 8 party favors. How many party favors are there in all?

6. Write the number that is 200 more than the product of 6 and 3,950.

Name _____

Bar Graphs

Essential Question How can you draw a bar graph to show data in a table or picture graph?

Learning Objective You will create a scaled bar graph to represent a data set given in a table or a picture graph.

Unlock the Problem (Real World) (Hands On)

Andre took a survey of his classmates' favorite team sports. He recorded the results in the tables at the right. How can he show the results in a bar graph?

Favorite Team Sport

Sport		Tally
Soccer	⚽	IIII IIII II
Basketball	🏀	IIII
Baseball	⚾	IIII IIII IIII
Football	🏈	IIII IIII

Favorite Team Sport

Soccer	12
Basketball	4
Baseball	14
Football	9

Make a bar graph.

STEP 1

Write a title at the top to tell what the graph is about. Label the side of the graph to tell about the bars. Label the bottom of the graph to explain what the numbers tell.

STEP 2

Choose numbers for the bottom of the graph so that most of the bars will end on a line. Since the least number is 4 and the greatest number is 14, make the scale 0–16. Mark the scale by twos.

STEP 3

Draw and shade a bar to show the number for each sport.

Math Talk

Process Standards 6

Make Connections How did you know how long to draw the bar for each of the sports?

Oliver's school is having a walk-a-thon to raise money for the school library. Oliver made a picture graph to show the number of miles some students walked. Use the picture graph to complete the frequency table. Then, make a bar graph of Oliver's data. Use a scale of 0–_____, and mark the scale by _____.

School Walk-a-Thon	
Chloe	👕 👕 👕 👕 👕
Oliver	👕 👕 🕴
Levi	👕
Maya	👕 👕 👕 👕

Key: Each 👕 = 2 miles.

School Walk-a-Thon	
Chloe	
Oliver	
Levi	
Maya	

Use your bar graph for 1–4.

1. Which student walked the most miles? _____

   Think: Which student's bar is the tallest?

2. How many more miles would Oliver have had to walk to equal the number of miles Maya walked? _____

3. How many miles did the students walk? _____

4. Write the number of miles the students walked in order from greatest to least. _____

Math Talk

Process Standards ③

Apply How would the graph have to change if another student, Troy, walked double the number of miles Maya walked?

Name _____

5. Avery and Elijah did an experiment with a spinner. Avery recorded the result of each spin in the table at the right. Use the tally table to complete the frequency table. Then, use the data in the table to make a bar graph. Choose numbers and a scale and decide how to mark your graph.

Spinner Results	
Color	**Tally**
Red	卌 |||
Yellow	卌 卌 卌	
Blue	卌 卌
Green	卌 卌 ||

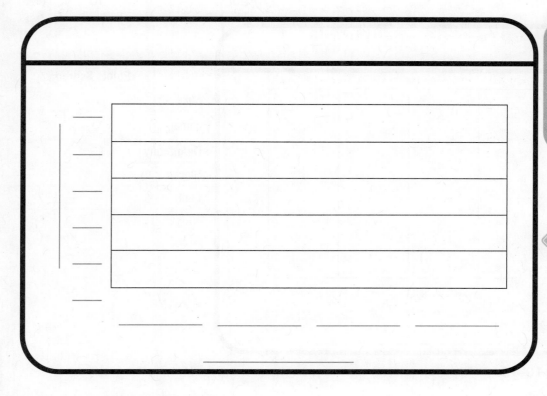

Spinner Results	
Red	
Yellow	
Blue	
Green	

ERROR Alert

Be sure to draw the bars correctly when you transfer data from a table.

Use your bar graph for 6–8.

6. The pointer stopped on _____ half the number

of times that it stopped on _____ .

7. [GO DEEPER] The pointer stopped on green _____ fewer times than it stopped on blue and yellow combined.

8. [PROCESS STANDARDS 6] **Explain** why you chose the scale you did.

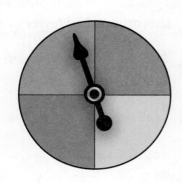

_____

_____

Problem Solving • Applications Real World

9. **PROCESS STANDARDS 4** **Use Graphs** Alexis recorded the number of points some basketball players scored. Use the table at the right to complete the tally table. Then, use the data in the table to make a bar graph. Choose a scale so that most of the bars will end on a line.

Points Scored	
Player	**Number of Points**
Mike	10
Jamal	30
DeAnthony	15
Steven	20
Paul	10

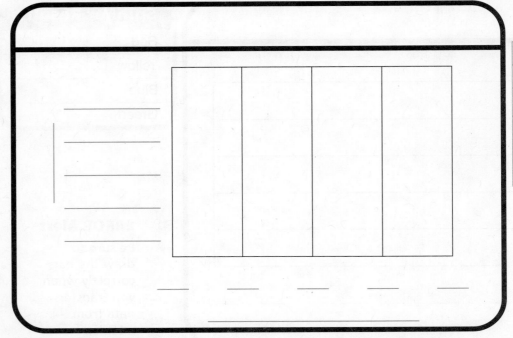

Points Scored	
Mike	
Jamal	
DeAnthony	
Steven	
Paul	

Use your bar graph for 10–12.

10. **GO DEEPER** Which player scored more points than DeAnthony but fewer points than Jamal? _____

11. **THINK SMARTER** Write and solve a new question that matches the data in your bar graph.

_____

_____

12. **THINK SMARTER** Which player scored 10 fewer points than Steven?

Name _____

Bar Graphs

Ben asked some friends to name their favorite breakfast food. He recorded their choices in the frequency table below.

Learning Objective You will create a scaled bar graph to represent a data set given in a table or a picture graph.

1. Use the frequency table to complete the tally table.

Favorite Breakfast Food	
Food	Number of Votes
Waffles	8
Cereal	14
Pancakes	12
Oatmeal	4

Favorite Breakfast Food	
Waffles	
Cereal	
Pancakes	
Oatmeal	

2. Complete the bar graph by using Ben's data.

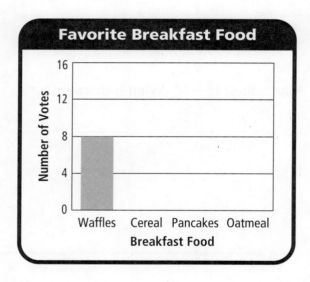

Use your bar graph for 3–5.

3. Which food did the most people choose as their favorite breakfast food?

   _____

4. How many more people chose waffles and pancakes than cereal and oatmeal?

   _____

5. Suppose 3 people changed their minds and voted for waffles instead of cereal. How would you change the bar graph?

   _____

   _____

6. **WRITE** ▸ *Math* Use the data on page 94 and explain how to draw a bar for a player named Kevin who scored 20 points.

   _____

   _____

Lesson Check

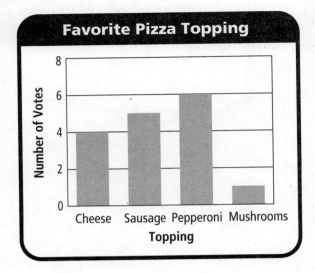

Favorite Pizza Topping

1. Bentley asked his friends to name their favorite pizza topping. He recorded the results in a bar graph. How many people chose sausage?

_____

2. Suppose 3 more friends chose cheese. Where would the bar for cheese end?

_____

Spiral Review

3. Find the sum.

$$\begin{array}{r} 458 \\ + 214 \\ \hline \end{array}$$

_____

4. Matt added $1\frac{2}{3} + 3\frac{1}{2}$. What is this sum?

_____

5. There are 682 runners registered for an upcoming race. What is 682 rounded to the nearest hundred?

_____

6. What is the name of the quadrilateral that has at exactly 1 pair of parallel sides?

_____

Circle Graphs

Essential Question How can you interpret data that is displayed in a circle graph?

Learning Objective You will interpret data that is displayed in a circle graph.

Use a **circle graph** to show data as parts of a whole. You can use a circle graph to compare data about different groups.

Unlock the Problem

Michelle took a survey of favorite summer activities. She recorded her data in a circle graph. Which activity received the most votes?

Favorite Summer Activity				
Activity	Hiking	Fishing	Going to the Beach	Visiting a Theme Park
Votes	4	3	4	5

Each color represents an activity.

The number of equal sections shows the number of people Michelle surveyed.

The circle represents the whole, or all the activities.

_____ has the greatest amount shaded.

So, _____ received the _____ votes.

- How is a circle graph like a bar graph? How is it different?

_____

_____

Math Talk

Process Standards ④

Use Graphs Explain what the whole circle in the graph represents.

🔵 Examples Interpret a circle graph.

A Johnny and his classmates are having a pizza party at school. His teacher took a survey of what type of pizza they would like and recorded the data in a circle graph.

Favorite Pizza	
Type	**Votes**
Pepperoni	15
Cheese	25
Spinach	10

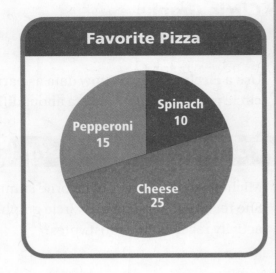

1. Which type of pizza was least popular?

   Think: Which section of the graph is the smallest?

   _____

2. How many more students voted for pepperoni and cheese combined than for spinach?

   _____

3. Which type of pizza received $\frac{1}{2}$ of the votes?

   _____

B Hiro asked his classmates what their favorite breakfast food was. He made a circle graph to record their votes.

4. Did waffles, eggs, or cereal receive the most votes?

   _____

5. What type of breakfast received the second greatest number of votes?

   _____

6. Which type of breakfast received less than $\frac{1}{4}$ of the votes?

   _____

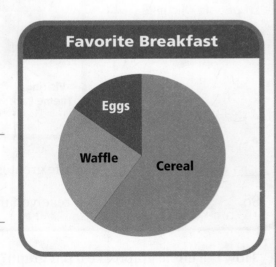

Name _____

How Do You Get to School?

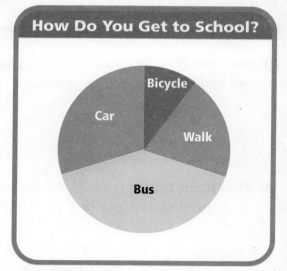

Use the graph for 1–3.

1. What is the most common way of getting to school?

_____

✓ 2. What is the least common way of getting to school?

_____

✓ 3. Do more students get to school by car or by walking?

_____

Math Talk Process Standards ①

Explain how you know that more students took the bus to school than walked.

On Your Own

Use the Favorite Fruit graph for 4–6.

4. Which fruit received the greatest number of votes?

_____

5. How many more people voted for oranges than pears?

_____

6. If 14 more people were surveyed and 7 chose apples, how many votes for apples would there be?

_____

Favorite Fruit

Apples 2, Pears 6, Oranges, 12

Use the Favorite Dog graph for 7–9.

7. Which dog received the least number of votes?

_____

8. Which dog received almost half of the votes?

_____

9. Which two dogs received about the same number of votes?

_____

Favorite Dog

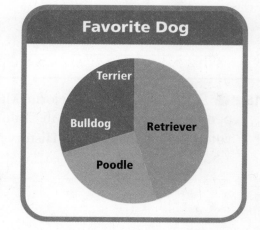

Terrier, Bulldog, Retriever, Poodle

Problem Solving • Applications

Use the Favorite Museum graph for 10–12.

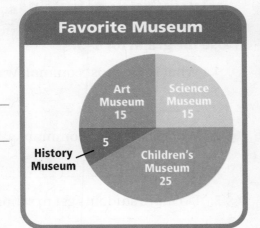

Favorite Museum

10. How can you use the circle graph to find which museum received the most votes?

_____

_____

11. How many more people chose the Children's Museum than the History Museum?

_____

12. How many people were surveyed?_____

13. **THINK SMARTER** **What's the Error?** Joey earns $1 on Monday, $4 on Wednesday, and $5 on Friday. He says Graph A matches the data. Describe Joey's error. Tell which graph matches the set of data.

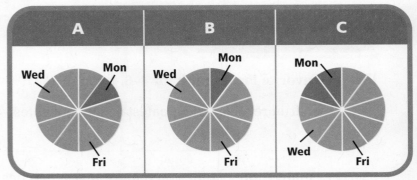

_____

_____

14. **GO DEEPER** Raymond's allowance is $10. He spends $5 for a movie ticket and $2 on snacks. He saves the rest. How would you show this data in a circle graph?

_____

_____

15. **THINK SMARTER** Use the Favorite Museum graph. How many more people voted for the Art and Children's Museums combined than voted for the Science and History Museums combined?

_____

Circle Graphs

Learning Objective You will interpret data that is displayed in a circle graph.

Use the Favorite Type of Pet graph for 1–3.

1. Which pet received the most votes?

   Think: Which section of the graph is the largest?

   _____ dogs _____

2. Did cats or fish receive more votes?

   _____

3. Which pet received the same number of votes as birds?

   _____

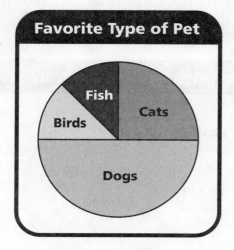

Favorite Type of Pet

Use the Cafeteria Survey graph for 4–5.

4. The manager of a school cafeteria surveyed students to find out what item they would like to see added to the school's lunch menu. The circle graph shows the results. How many students voted?

   _____

5. How many more students voted for enchiladas than stir fry and chicken salad combined?

   _____

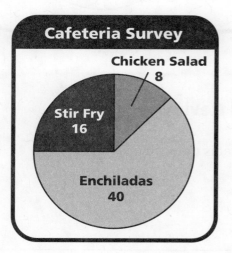

Cafeteria Survey

Problem Solving Real World

6. Use the Cafeteria Survey graph above. Which two school lunches combined received a total of 48 votes?

7. **WRITE** ▸ *Math* Explain what you can tell just by comparing the sections in the Favorite Type of Pet circle graph above.

   _____

   _____

   _____

   _____

Lesson Check

Jamal surveyed students about their favorite type of comic book. The results are shown in the circle graph.

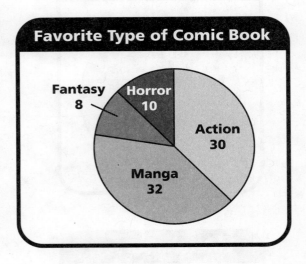

Favorite Type of Comic Book

Fantasy 8
Horror 10
Action 30
Manga 32

Use the Favorite Type of Comic Book graph for 1–2.

1. Which type of comic book received the greatest number of votes?

   _____

2. How many fewer votes did fantasy comic books receive than action comic books received?

   _____

Spiral Review

3. What is the sum of $2\frac{4}{5} + 1\frac{1}{3}$?

   _____

4. What are the factors of 36?

   _____

5. It takes 2 cups of pancake batter to make 8 pancakes. How much batter is needed to make 24 pancakes?

   (A) 6 cups   (C) 18 cups
   (B) 8 cups   (D) 24 cups

6. Mark has a collection of 14 action figures. He wants to increase his collection to be three times as great as it is now. How many action figures does Mark want in his collection?

   (A) 28   (C) 36
   (B) 32   (D) 42

Math and Science Skills

Use with *ScienceFusion*
pages 22–23.

Develop Concepts

1. Suppose you are a space scientist who wants to send a robot to Mars to test soil samples. How might you use math?

_____

_____

_____

2. Suppose you are a weather scientist. How would you use numbers in your investigations?

_____

_____

_____

Develop Inquiry Skills

3. Which estimated whale populations are the smallest and the largest?

_____

_____

_____

4. How can you tell that these numbers are all estimates?

_____

_____

_____

Do the Math!

5. Complete the table with the data from the whale populations table. List the whales in order from least population to greatest population. Then find how much less the whale population for one kind of whale is compared to the whale with the next greatest population.

Kind of Whale	Population	Amount Greater than Previous Whale Population
Blue whale	14,000	N/A
Humpback whale	40,000	26,000

6. Which two kinds of whales have a population that is the closest to one another? Explain your answer.

_____

_____

7. How much greater is the greatest population than the least population? How did you find it?

_____

_____

Summarize

8. What skills do you use in math and science?

_____

_____

_____

Heat Proofing a Home

Use with *ScienceFusion* pages 210–211.

Develop Concepts

1. Why do you think a specific gas is used instead of air?

_____

_____

_____

2. What are some ways that we keep heat from coming into our homes when the weather is hot and leaving our homes when the weather is cold?

_____

_____

_____

Develop Inquiry Skills

3. Why are basements usually cool year-round?

_____

_____

_____

4. How might you eliminate the need to air-condition your house, even in the hottest weather?

_____

_____

_____

Do the Math!

5. Complete the table with the data on the Ogburn family's plan to heat proof their house.

Action	Savings per year	Cost
Adding insulation	$	$400
Wrapping pipes	$	$100
Buying new windows	$	$10,500
Total	$	$

6. About how much more money will replacing the windows save each year than wrapping the water pipes? Justify your answer mathematically.

_____

_____

7. In how many years will the savings pay for the cost of these home improvements? Explain your answer.

_____

_____

Summarize

8. What causes heat transfer, and how can you reduce it?

_____

_____

_____

_____

The Food Eaters

Use with *ScienceFusion*
pages 444–445.

Develop Inquiry Skills

1. How does the amount of food that the animal eats relate to how much it weighs? Is anything surprising?

_____

_____

_____

2. Which animal is most likely to have more changes in its diet during the year? Explain.

_____

_____

_____

Develop Vocabulary

3. Define the following terms in your own words.

Consumer: _____

_____

_____

Producer: _____

_____

_____

Do the Math!

4. Complete the table to find the fraction of an animal's body weight that it eats each day. The numerator is how much the animal eats and the denominator is how much the animal weighs.

Animal	How Much It Eats a Day	How Much It Weighs	Fraction of Its Body Weight	Rank (1 is greatest fraction)
Giant panda	20 kg	160 kg		
Giraffe	25 kg	1,250 kg		
Blue whale	7 metric tons	180 metric tons		

5. Which animal eats the highest fraction of its body weight of food every day? Least?

_____

_____

_____

6. How many kilograms of food would 18 giraffes eat? Show your work.

_____

_____

_____

Summarize

7. What is a consumer? Give some examples.

_____

_____

_____

Fast or Slow?

Use with *ScienceFusion*
pages 268–269.

Develop Vocabulary

1. Define the following terms in your own words.

Speed: _____

_____

_____

Velocity: _____

_____

_____

Develop Concepts

2. What does the number line show? Which animal traveled the farthest?

_____

_____

_____

3. Which animal was the fastest? Which animal was the slowest?
   How do you know?

_____

_____

_____

Do the Math!

4. Complete the table with the data on the distance traveled for the turtle, cat, and rabbit. Divide the distance traveled by the time to calculate the speed of the animal.

Animal	Distance Traveled (meters)	Time (seconds)	Speed (meters per second)
Rabbit		10	
Turtle		10	
Cat		10	

5. Which animal was the fastest? List the animals in order from the slowest to the fastest.

_____

_____

_____

6. A chicken joins the race and runs at 4 meters per second. How far would the chicken run in 10 seconds?

_____

_____

Summarize

7. Compare speed and velocity.

_____

_____

_____

Flash and Boom!

Use with *ScienceFusion*
pages 176–177.

Develop Concepts

1. The sun is Earth's main source of light energy. How else do we get light energy?

_____

_____

_____

2. How is sound made? How can you describe sound?

_____

_____

_____

Develop Inquiry Skills

3. Which instruments are most alike? Explain.

_____

_____

_____

4. How are the drum and saxophone alike?

_____

_____

_____

Do the Math!

5. Complete the table to show how far away lightning is based on the time between seeing the lightning and hearing the thunder.

Time (sec)	35	20	40		15	
Distance (mi)				10		6

6. There are 15 seconds from the time you see lightning to the time you hear thunder. How far away is the lightning? Explain how you found your answer.

_____

_____

_____

7. Lightning is 60 miles away. How many seconds will there be between seeing the lightning and hearing the thunder? Explain how you found your answer.

_____

_____

Summarize

8. How are light and sound alike? How are they different?

_____

_____

_____

What Goes Up Must Come Down

Use with *ScienceFusion*
pages 348–349.

Develop Vocabulary

1. Define the following terms in your own words.

   Condensation: _____

   _____

   _____

   Precipitation: _____

   _____

   _____

Develop Concepts

2. What happens to all water on Earth?

   _____

   _____

   _____

3. Imagine you are a raindrop falling to Earth's surface. Describe your path through the water cycle.

   _____

   _____

   _____

   _____

Do the Math!

4. Complete the table with the sizes of droplets and dust particles compared to a raindrop. Then, rank their sizes from 1–4 with 1 being the smallest.

Object	Fraction of a Raindrop	Rank
Average droplet		
Raindrop		
Dust particle		
Large droplet		

5. How do you know which fraction is the smallest? The largest?

_____

_____

_____

6. Another droplet is $\frac{1}{50}$ the size of a raindrop. Write all of the fractions, including this one, from largest to smallest.

_____

_____

_____

Summarize

7. What are the stages of the water cycle?

_____

_____

_____

Name _____

Bringing Up Baby

Use with *ScienceFusion* pages 502–505.

Develop Inquiry Skills

1. What visual clues in the picture tell you that an alligator's eggs are soft and leathery instead of hard and brittle?

_____

_____

_____

2. Compare and contrast the life cycle of a penguin and a kangaroo.

_____

_____

_____

Develop Concepts

3. Animals that feed their young are called mammals. What other animals do you know that feed they young milk?

_____

_____

_____

4. How do young animals that are not mammals get fed?

_____

_____

_____

Do the Math!

5. Raccoons usually give birth to 3 to 5 young at a time. Raccoons give birth only once a year. Suppose a female raccoon lives 10 years. She is able to give birth for 9 of those years. Complete the table to show possible numbers of offspring that a female raccoon can have in her lifetime.

	Year 1	Year 2	Year 3	Year 4	Year 5	Year 6	Year 7	Year 8	Year 9	Total
3 babies										
5 babies										

6. How many offspring will she have? Explain how you found the answer.

_____

_____

_____

7. Why is there not an exact answer?

_____

_____

_____

Summarize

8. Compare the life cycles of the following groups of organisms: turtles and penguins, cats and kangaroos, or bluebirds and deer?

_____

_____

_____

Generating Electricity

Use with *ScienceFusion*
pages 250–251.

Develop Concepts

1. What might happen if people don't conserve electricity?

_____

_____

_____

2. What are some ways that you, personally, can conserve electricity?

_____

_____

_____

Develop Vocabulary

3. Define the following terms in your own words.

Generator: _____

_____

_____

Do the Math!

4. Complete the table with the data on Sam's electricity bill.

Animal	Fraction of Bill	Amount (in dollars)
Air Conditioner	$\frac{1}{2}$	
Water Heater	$\frac{1}{5}$	
Other		

5. How much did it cost to run everything besides the air conditioner and the water heater? Explain how you found your answer.

_____

_____

_____

6. What might be included in "other"?

_____

_____

_____

Summarize

7. Why is it important to conserve electricity?

_____

_____

_____

Name _____

The Good and the Bad of It

Use with *ScienceFusion* pages 92–93.

Develop Concepts

1. Why do people want different kinds of light bulbs?

_____

_____

_____

2. Do all light bulbs serve a practical purpose?

_____

_____

_____

Develop Inquiry Skills

3. Before airplanes were invented, in what other ways did people travel long distances? Were these ways better or worse than flying?

_____

_____

_____

4. What are some examples of new problems caused by the invention of airplanes?

_____

_____

_____

© Houghton Mifflin Harcourt Publishing Company

Do the Math!

Complete the table using the Light Bulb Cost Comparison chart. Then use the data in the table to answer the questions below.

Light Bulb Cost Comparisons		
	25-Watt CFL	100-Watt Incandescent
Cost of bulb	$3.40	
Bulb life	1,667 days (4.5 years)	
Energy cost per year	$6.00	
Total cost over 4.5 years	$27.00	

5. How much more is the total cost of an incandescent bulb than a CFL? How much would your yearly energy cost be if you had 20 CFL bulbs in your home? Which bulb lasts longer?

_____

_____

6. How can you tell which bulb is better for the bulb life? For the total cost over 4.5 years? Explain your answer.

_____

_____

7. Costs are usually written as decimals. Write the following costs from the table using fractions instead of decimals: 3.40, 0.60, 118.50.

_____

_____

Summarize

8. What is the connection between technology growth, new problems, and further technology growth?

_____

_____

_____

You Have a Solution

Use with *ScienceFusion* pages 156–157.

Develop Vocabulary

1. Define the following terms in your own words.

Solution: _____

_____

_____

Solvent: _____

_____

_____

Develop Concepts

2. Do the pepper and water make a solution? Explain your answer.

_____

_____

_____

_____

3. Do the salt and water make a solution? Explain your answer.

_____

_____

_____

_____

Do the Math!

4. Complete the table. Find the amount of sugar or water needed for each solution.

Substance	Ratio	Solution 1	Solution 2	Solution 3
Sugar	210 g	g	g	1,050 g
Water	100 ml	200 ml	700 ml	ml

5. Explain how you found the number of grams of sugar when you knew the number of milliliters of water.

_____

_____

_____

6. How much water will it take to dissolve 1,050 g of sugar? Explain your answer.

_____

_____

_____

Summarize

7. How are solutions and mixtures alike? How are they different?

_____

_____

_____

Name _____

Other Models Scientists Use

Use with *ScienceFusion* pages 54–55.

Develop Concepts

1. What kinds of toys are used to build three-dimensional models?

_____

_____

_____

_____

2. Why might you choose to use a computer model instead of a physical model?

_____

_____

_____

_____

Develop Vocabulary

3 . Define the following terms in your own words.

Three-dimensional model: _____

_____

_____

Computer model: _____

_____

_____

Do the Math!

4. Complete the table with the data for the model of the solar system. Use whole numbers, fractions, or mixed numbers to estimate the size of Earth compared to each object.

Planet	Diameter (mm)	Diameter compared to Earth
Sun	1,100	
Mercury	4	
Venus	9	$\frac{9}{10}$
Earth	10	$\frac{1}{1}$
Mars	5	
Jupiter	110	
Saturn	92	
Uranus	37	
Neptune	36	

5. Which fractions tell the sizes of Mars, Venus, and Mercury compared to Earth?

_____

_____

6. Which object is 11 times the diameter of Earth? Which object is about 9 times the diameter of Earth?

_____

Summarize

7. What are some different kinds of models, and why do we use them?

_____

_____

Name _____

Night and Day

Develop Concepts

Use with *ScienceFusion* pages 398–399.

1. Why do you see different things at different times?

_____

_____

_____

2. How does facing different directions model day and night?

_____

_____

_____

Develop Vocabulary

3. Define the following terms in your own words.

Rotates: _____

_____

_____

Axis: _____

_____

_____

Do the Math!

4. Complete the table with the data to find the difference between a day on Earth and a day on other planets.

Planet	Day	Day on Earth	Difference	Shorter/ Longer than Earth Day
Mercury	59 Earth days			
Jupiter	9 Earth hours, 55 minutes			
Neptune	16 Earth hours, 6 minutes			

5. How did you know which value to use for an Earth day: 1 day or 24 hours?

_____

_____

_____

6. A new planet is discovered. Its day is 4 Earth days, 17 hours, 43 minutes long. What is the difference between its day and an Earth day? Is it longer or shorter than an Earth day?

_____

_____

_____

Summarize

7. What causes day and night?

_____

_____

_____

Name _____

Pump Up the Volume!

Use with *ScienceFusion* pages 116–117.

Develop Vocabulary

1. Define the following term in your own words.

Volume: _____

_____

Develop Concepts

2. What causes the difference in the two volume measurements, with and without your object?

_____

_____

3. How can you use the two measurements to find the volume of the object?

_____

_____

Interpret Visuals

4. How much water pushed out of the tub when the dog is put in it?

_____

_____

5. Would more or less water be pushed out by a smaller dog? Why?

_____

_____

Do the Math!

5. The surface area is the sum of the areas of each face of a rectangular prism. Complete the table with the data about the surface area and volume of a rectangular solid.

Rectangular Prism	5 cm × 4 cm × 2 cm	3 cm × 3 cm × 3 cm
Area of top (square cm)		
Area of bottom (square cm)		
Area of left (square cm)		
Area of right (square cm)		
Area of front (square cm)		
Area of back (square cm)		

6. What patterns do you see when finding the areas of each face of a rectangular prism?

_____

_____

7. Complete the table to find the volume.

Rectangular Prism	5 cm × 4 cm × 2 cm	3 cm × 3 cm × 3 cm
Volume (cubic cm)		

8. Compare finding the area of a face of a rectangular prism and the prism's volume.

_____

_____

Summarize

8. What is volume? How can you find the volume of an irregularly-shaped object?

_____

_____

_____